CW00573365

Suffolk

WALKS

Compiled by
John Brooks
Revised by
Dennis and
Jan Kelsall

JARROLD
publishing

Text:	John Brooks
	Revised text for 2007 edition, Dennis and Jan Kelsall
Photography:	John Brooks, Jarrold Publishing and Dennis Kelsall
Editorial:	Ark Creative (UK) Ltd.
Design:	Ark Creative (UK) Ltd.

Series Consultant: Brian Conduit

OS Ordnance Survey® This product includes mapping data licensed from Ordnance Survey® with the permission of the Controller of Her Majesty's Stationery Office. © Crown Copyright 2007. All rights reserved. Licence number 100017593. Ordnance Survey, the OS symbol and Pathfinder are registered trademarks and Explorer, Landranger and Outdoor Leisure are trademarks of the Ordnance Survey, the national mapping agency of Great Britain.

Jarrold Publishing   ISBN 978-0-7117-1597-4

While every care has been taken to ensure the accuracy of the route directions, the publishers cannot accept responsibility for errors or omissions, or for changes in details given. The countryside is not static: hedges and fences can be removed, field boundaries can alter, footpaths can be rerouted and changes in ownership can result in the closure or diversion of some concessionary paths. Also, paths that are easy and pleasant for walking in fine conditions may become slippery, muddy and difficult in wet weather, while stepping stones across rivers and streams may become impassable.

If you find an inaccuracy in either the text or maps, please write to or e-mail Jarrold Publishing at the addresses below.

First published 2001
by Jarrold Publishing
Revised and reprinted 2005 and 2007.

Printed in Singapore. 3/07

Jarrold Publishing
Pathfinder Guides, Healey House, Dene Road, Andover, Hampshire SP10 2AA
email: info@totalwalking.co.uk
www.totalwalking.co.uk

Front cover: Dunwich
Previous page: Lavenham

Contents

The National Trust; The Ramblers' Association; Walkers and the Law; Countryside Access Charter; Global Positioning System (GPS); Walking Safety; Useful Organisations; Ordnance Survey Maps

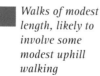

■ Short, easy walks

■ Walks of modest length, likely to involve some modest uphill walking

■ More challenging walks which may be longer and/or over more rugged terrain, often with some stiff climbs

Keymap

Walk	Page	Start	Nat. Grid Reference	Distance	Time
Barham, Baylham and Coddenham	62	Gipping Valley Centre, Barham Picnic Site	TM 123512	8 miles (12.9km)	3½ hrs
Carlton Marshes and the River Waveney	12	Carlton Marshes Visitor Centre, Carlton Colville	TM 508920	2¾ miles (4.4km)	1 hr
Constable Country — Flatford and East Bergholt	33	East Bergholt	TM 069346	5½ miles (8.9km)	2½ hrs
Covehithe and Benacre	24	Covehithe	TM 521818	5½ miles (8.9km)	2½ hrs
Cretingham and Brandeston	36	Oak Corner, Cretingham	TM 227603	5 miles (8km)	2 hrs
Darmsden and the Gipping valley	18	Needham Lake, Needham Market	TM 093546	4¼ miles (6.8km)	2 hrs
Denham Castle and the three churches	69	Packhorse Bridge, Moulton	TL 697645	9¼ miles (14.9km)	4 hrs
Dingle Marshes from Dunwich	20	Dunwich beach	TM 478706	4¼ miles (6.8km)	2½ hrs
Eye and Braiseworth	30	Eye	TM 145738	5 miles (8km)	2 hrs
Framlingham from Dennington	38	Dennington church	TM 281670	6¼ miles (10.1km)	2½ hrs
Glemsford from Clare via Cavendish	82	Clare Country Park	TL 770451	11½ miles (18.5km)	5 hrs
Iken and Tunstall Forest	55	Snape Maltings	TM 391575	8 miles (12.9km)	3½ hrs
Kersey and Lindsey Castle from Hadleigh	73	Toppesfield Bridge, Hadleigh	TM 025421	9½ miles (15.3km)	4 hrs
Long Melford from Lavenham	86	Lavenham	TL 913489	12¾ miles (20.5km)	5½ hrs
Nowton Park and High Suffolk	26	Nowton Park, Bury St Edmunds	TL 864621	4½ miles (7.2km)	2 hrs
Orford coast and country	41	Orford	TM 424496	6¼ miles (10.1km)	2½ hrs
Pakenham Mills from Ixworth	14	Ixworth	TL 931703	5 miles (8km)	2 hrs
Saxmundham, Kelsale and the Gull Stream	49	Saxmundham	TM 386632	7 miles (11.3km)	3 hrs
Shingle Street and Alderton	22	Coastguard cottages, Shingle Street	TM 369431	4½ miles (7.2km)	2½ hrs
Shotley Peninsula	76	Shotley	TM 235350	10¼ miles (16.5km)	4½ hrs
Somerleyton and Waddling Lane	52	Duke's Head pub, Somerleyton	TM 478971	6¼ miles (10.1km)	2½ hrs
Southwold	16	Southwold pier	TM 511767	3¼ miles (6km)	1½ hrs
Stowlangtoft and Norton from Pakenham	66	Pakenham church	TL 930670	9¼ miles (14.9km)	4 hrs
Sutton Hoo, Shottisham and the River Deben	79	Sutton Heath picnic site	TM 305474	10 miles (16.1km)	4 hrs
Thorpeness from Leiston	46	Leiston Leisure Centre	TM 451619	6½ miles (10.5km)	3½ hrs
Wenhaston and Mells from Blythburgh	58	Blythburgh	TM 450752	8¼ miles (13.3km)	3½ hrs
West Row and Worlington from Mildenhall	44	Mildenhall	TL 712744	6¼ miles (10.1km)	2½ hrs
West Stow, forest and riverside	28	Forest Lodge Picnic Site, West Stow	TL 815714	5¼ miles (8.4km)	2½ hrs

Comments

A delightful beginning by lakes and riverside before the way crosses the busy A14 and climbs through woodland to beautiful Coddenham. The way back is through parkland surrounding Shrubland Hall.

This walk through marshland south of Lowestoft reaches an isolated section of the bank of the River Waveney. The return passes Sprat's Water — a wonderful habitat for reedbed birds.

Connoisseurs of the English landscape flock to Dedham Vale to try to recognise features that Constable painted. This walk passes one of his most famous viewpoints as well as Flatford Mill itself.

The coastline between Covehithe and Benacre suffers badly from erosion and uprooted tree stumps scattered on the beach attest to the incessant march of the sea. Benacre Broad is an RSPB reserve.

The beautiful landscape of the upper River Deben is well seen in this circuit beginning in the pleasant village of Cretingham. There is an excellent selection of footpaths serving this neighbourhood.

Climb to the windswept countryside above Needham Market and then descend to the sheltered bank of the River Gipping, a delightful waterway that is the haunt of herons, kingfishers and otters.

'The Three Churches Walk' has long been famous and is a fine way of sampling the scenery in the west of the county. Although little remains of Denham Castle this part provides magnificent views.

The outward part of the walk is by the shore but the route turns inland after a couple of miles to cross reedbeds and reach a sandy ridge covered by pine trees that makes a delightful contrast.

Eye is a country town isolated from main roads. The church and castle and other fine buildings reflect its former importance, and the walk shows the best of the surrounding countryside.

Dennington and Framlingham both have magnificent churches and the latter also has a splendid castle. The walk uses footpaths that sometimes cross cropped land.

Three of Suffolk's most famous villages are included on a route following the upper valley of the River Stour. A choice of tearooms and pubs is available for refreshment on the way.

This will be a favourite walk with many people as it combines a lovely estuary section with a return through equally attractive forest. It is an excellent all season route.

None of Suffolk's 'chocolate box villages' is more famous or picturesque than Kersey. The walk is a satisfying ramble covering a wide tract of farmland. Spare time to see Hadleigh's medieval buildings.

Even though the county is virtually gradient-free you will feel a sense of accomplishment on completing this lengthy walk. It visits two showpiece villages and passes through delightful landscapes.

Walking in a public park often gives little pleasure, but Nowton Park on the edge of Bury St Edmunds is a shining exception. An interesting stretch of footpath is a prelude to a return through the park.

Orford was a busy seaport until the 17th century when its river began to be choked by silt. The castle is often in view during the walk. Dating from 1165 it is polygonal – a revolutionary design at the time.

This short walk starts at Ixworth and is on bridleways and quiet lanes. It goes across lonely country-side and by two lovely mills, one powered by the wind, the other by water.

The walk follows an attractive stream to the lakes at its source. It then passes through the quiet village of Kelsale, where the lychgate is one of the most unusual in the country.

One can easily imagine smugglers and wreckers of bygone days on the beach at Shingle Street. The walk uses the flood wall and field paths to take you to Alderton and its pub.

The estuaries of the Stour and Orwell embrace the Shotley peninsula close to Ipswich. At weekends the rivers are crowded with boats which give the walk extra colour and interest.

Somerleyton is one of the most attractive Broadland villages, its pretty cottages matching the architecture of Somerleyton Hall. The walk is on tracks and paths around the outskirts of the estate.

There are many good reasons to visit Southwold, not least its interesting buildings and promenade beach huts, whilst fresh fish is sold from fishermen's kiosks beside the river.

Small villages with unpretentious churches feature here, where you wander past fields of wheat, barley and sugar beet. If anything is typical of rural Suffolk it is lovely countryside like this.

Birdwatchers and archaeologists will enjoy the heath and estuary, whilst the path along the cliffs above the Deben gives fine views. There is an opportunity to visit the Sutton Hoo exhibition.

This walk is a good mix of seaside and countryside, the former following the coast path from Sizewell to Thorpeness while the latter is mainly on field paths over heath and arable land.

You are unlikely to meet other walkers on these paths in the valley of the River Blyth.

Suffolk's western boundary lies in fenland, which is sometimes unfairly dismissed as being un-interesting. Those who tackle this route will find the River Lark delightful and the horizons immense.

Forest, sandy field tracks, timbered parkland and quiet riverside are combined to illustrate the varied landscapes of Breckland in north west Suffolk.

At-a-glance...

Introduction to Suffolk

Suffolk is a reticent county. Its landscapes are never spectacular and may, in a few places in the midst of its prairie-like corn belt, lack character. Yet the riverside meadows of the Stour valley are the ones that Constable painted and they remain as beautiful today as when he portrayed them two centuries ago. In the same way, Suffolk's lonely expanses of estuarine marsh, which are a feature of the coast, have a quality that appeals to writers as well as artists – here you realise the importance of the sky in East Anglian scenery.

The evolution of the countryside

Suffolk is the easternmost county of England with an area of 1,466 sq miles (3,797 sq km), a population of 669,000, and a highest point just 128m (420ft) above sea level. Oak forest veiled much of its countryside until the 18th century, but most of this fell to axe and saw when the navy had to enlarge its fleet against the threat posed by Napoleon.

More or less coincidentally with the felling of the forest, Acts of Inclosure enabled landowners to enlarge their estates by taking over common lands. These had supplied free grazing and firewood for generations of villagers so when the privileges were withdrawn many of them were left destitute. Some emigrated to America and Australia while others took work in the emerging industrial towns.

The agricultural depression of the 1930s saw many more people forced from their land. This time it affected farmers who had for long struggled to make a living from a few acres of small fields bounded by sturdy hedges. Many of their farms were bought by neighbouring, wealthier landowners but Scottish farmers also took advantage of the low prices. Fields were merged to make units more suitable for cultivation by tractors and so began a process that has continued into the 21st century. Fortunately, we are beginning to recognise the damage to wildlife caused by removing ditches, ponds and hedges but there are many places in the county where above endless acres of grain or sugar beet the skylark no longer sings.

The buildings of Suffolk

The geology of the county is simple, with a dome of chalk having been covered by layers of different clays when the glaciers retreated at the end of the Ice Age. The clays suited deciduous woodland that provided the main landscape feature of inland Suffolk until the 18th century. These three ingredients provided the basic building materials that give Suffolk's ancient buildings their character.

Flints were mined from chalk and 'knapped' to produce dark hued building stone of uniform size. This is to be seen in the grander churches of the county, often worked into decorative panels with imported stone. More humble churches, and domestic and farm buildings, were often made of unworked flints picked from the fields or beach.

The various Suffolk clays were used for brickmaking from the 15th century, reviving a craft lost since Roman times. The county is particularly well endowed with brick-built mansions, and much brickwork is also to be seen in churches as well as in the castles at Orford and Framlingham.

The enduring quality of oak timber as a building material is seen all over Suffolk in exterior and interior work. Some of the most intricate examples of hammerbeam roofs are in Suffolk churches, those at Mildenhall and Needham Market being outstanding 'wooden visions of paradise'. The genius of Suffolk carpenters from different eras is also shown brilliantly at Dennington, where you may see a medieval carving of the Sciapod, a bizarre humanoid whose feet are as long as his body, with a Jacobean three decker pulpit and a fine set of box pews of 1725.

Suffolk has 500 medieval churches, and each has some important architectural or historical feature. The magnificence of churches such as those at Long Melford or Lavenham derives from local entrepreneurs who became wealthy by raising sheep or weaving the wool they produced. By endowing these wonderful churches the merchants hoped they would reap rewards in heaven. Certainly the generations that followed them have been grateful for the splendour created by the masons and carpenters.

Timber was also a vital ingredient in domestic architecture, as a visit to Lavenham or any other famously pretty village will show. Because of the considerable labour that was required to transform tree trunks into beams with relatively smooth edges, parts of the timber frame will probably have served other buildings before being used in the one where you see it today. The tree that it came from may have been felled 600 years ago. It is this sort of improvisation that makes the old houses of Suffolk so picturesque.

The ford in the village of Kersey

Writers, painters and a composer

The poetry of George Crabbe reflects the dire poverty suffered in rural Suffolk 200 or so years ago as well as the beauty of the landscape of east Suffolk. His verse appealed to another

Reedbeds are a common feature of the Suffolk landscape

Suffolk genius, Benjamin Britten, who set Crabbe's words to music in his opera *Peter Grimes*. The lonely salt marshes around Aldeburgh also inspired orchestral music such as the evocative *Sea Interludes*. The world famous concert hall that overlooks the marshes at Snape Maltings celebrates Benjamin Britten and is the venue for an outstanding annual music festival. The complex also provides facilities to encourage promising young musicians to develop their talents.

M.R. James used the same district as a setting for some of his ghost stories, and while walking along the deserted beach of Shingle Street or on the Dunwich marshes in the gloomy dusk of a November day it is easy to imagine being waylaid by the ghost of a smuggler. Anyone interested in the life of ordinary people in Suffolk in the 19th and early 20th centuries is recommended to read Ronald Blythe's *Akenfield*, a work written in the 1960s that has become a classic.

Of the many artists who have found inspiration in the Suffolk landscape two are immortal. John Constable was born at East Bergholt in 1776 and intended to be a portrait painter. However, he loved to paint landscapes and found inspiration for them in the everyday scenes that he saw in the Stour valley. He was thirty-five years old when his landscape of Dedham Vale made him known, and this was followed by further masterpieces such as *The Leaping Horse* and *The Hay Wain*. His work was never as popular in England as in France until after his death in 1827. Thomas Gainsborough was born in 1727 in Sudbury and trained in London before returning to Suffolk. Although most famous for his portraits of the rich and famous, Gainsborough's real passion was for landscapes and this must have derived from his upbringing in Suffolk.

Practical walking

With some 9,800 registered rights of way and a path network of more than 3,300 miles (5310km), Suffolk offers plenty of scope for countryside walking. Numerous long distance walks weave through the county and there is endless opportunity for shorter circular walks focusing on the places of interest and beauty spots that abound. Part of the Broads National Park lies within the boundaries of the county as well as two Areas of Outstanding Natural Beauty; Dedham Vale and Suffolk Coast and Heaths. Recent legislation has created many Access Areas, which includes extensive stretches of forest and heath. Such variety offers a wealth of different landscapes to explore.

The gentle, rolling terrain with few strenuous hills lends itself to undemanding walking, but this in no way diminishes the satisfaction to be gained from a day's ramble. Whilst the warnings that apply to upland or wilderness areas are here less relevant, a few simple, common-sense precautions will contribute to the comfort and pleasure of a day out. Rutted tracks, hidden rabbit holes, wet ground and tree roots are ever-present hazards and comfortable, waterproof boots that give support to the ankles are infinitely preferable to trainers or light shoes. As anywhere else in the country, the weather can be unpredictable and coastal winds may be unexpectedly cold, so it is always a good idea to carry waterproofs and something warm. During summer, suncream and a hat will guard against burning and a good supply of water or soft drink will help avoid the ill-effects of dehydration. On a fine day, the thought of shorts and T-shirts is often inviting, but more sensible are trousers and a sleeved shirt to protect against the nettles and brambles inevitably encountered during the summer months. Whilst many of the routes pass a refreshment stop during the course of the day, it is always a good idea to carry a snack to sustain you should your plans change or the pub be shut.

Suffolk's footpath officers and rangers work hard to keep the path network passable, but if you encounter an obstruction, damaged stile or gate, you will help their task by reporting it. There are contact numbers in the 'Further Information' section of this guide: the Broads Authority for within the National Park or the County Council elsewhere. Give a date and clear description of the problem with an accurate location, including a map reference if possible.

With the introduction of **'gps enabled' walks,** you will see that this book now includes a list of waypoints alongside the description of the walk. We have included these so that you can enjoy the full benefits of gps should you wish to. Gps is an amazingly useful and entertaining navigational aid, and you do not need to be computer literate to enjoy it.

GPS waypoint co-ordinates add value to your walk. You will now have the extra advantage of introducing 'direction' into your walking which will enhance your leisure walking and make it safer. Use of a gps brings greater confidence and security and you will find you cover ground a lot faster should you need to.

For more detailed information on using your gps, a *Pathfinder Guide* introducing you to gps and digital mapping is now available. *GPS for Walkers*, written by experienced gps teacher and navigation trainer Clive Thomas, is available in bookshops (ISBN 978-0-7117-4445-5) or order online at www.totalwalking.co.uk

Carlton Marshes and the River Waveney

		GPS waypoints
Start	Carlton Marshes Visitor Centre, Burnt Hill Lane, Carlton Colville	TM 508 920
Distance	2¾ miles (4.4km)	**A** TM 500 926
Approximate time	1 hour	**B** TM 494 930
Parking	Car park at start	**C** TM 493 927
Refreshments	Beverages available at visitor centre in season	**D** TM 503 916
Ordnance Survey maps	Landranger 134 (Norwich & The Broads), Explorer OL40 (The Broads)	

The Suffolk Wildlife Trust owns 100 acres (40ha) of grazing marshes, fen and peat pools within an area bounded by the River Waveney to the north and the railway to the south. It is an invaluable reserve reflecting all the different Broadland habitats within a compact area. The paths followed on the walk are all rights of way, though there is an interesting diversion to Sprat's Water towards the end of the walk for those without dogs.

The marshes are full of interest at any time of year but in winter it is a place to wrap up warmly - otherwise you will be in no doubt that Suffolk's east wind blows directly from the Urals. At the visitor centre you can find out about the rare varieties of plants, insects and birds that you may encounter here.

Turn right along the main track, passing through a gate onto the reserve. Over to the right are White Cast Marshes, where the Waveney flows into Oulton Broad. The reed beds are rigorously protected during the breeding season when marsh harriers nest. You might also hear the booming cry of the male bittern from the watery wilderness, a welcome sound heralding the comeback of this secretive bird. In 1997 there were only 11 breeding males left in the country, but extension and management of the reed beds had led to a five-fold increase by 2004.

In time the main track swings right towards Oulton Dyke **A**. Leave there, continuing ahead through a gate towards a cattle pen. Parting company with the grass track beyond it, walk to a stile in the far-right corner. Keep going with the ditch now on your left.

Peto's Marsh, to the right, takes its name from the Victorian railway magnate who rebuilt Somerleyton Hall. The vast expanse of cultivated land and grazing reflects the efficiency of the steam, diesel and electric pumps that in turn replaced the windmills, which first pumped water from dyke to river.

Steps lead up to the riverbank **B**, now well above the surrounding marshes, which have progressively sunk as a result of the drainage. Turn left beside

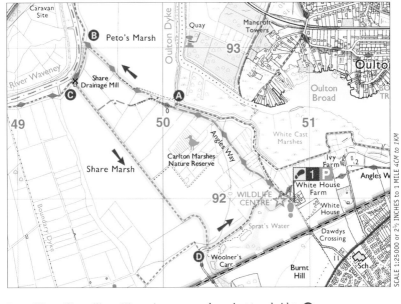

SCALE 1:25000 or 2½ INCHES to 1 MILE 4CM to 1KM

0	200	400	600	800 METRES	1
					KILOMETRES MILES
0	200	400	600 YARDS	½	

the Waveney, which in summer is busy with pleasure craft but utterly deserted during the winter months, shortly reaching a hardstanding, the site of the Share Drainage Mill. A hunk of metalwork is all that remains of the old water pump, its modern counterpart concealed within a low concrete bunker. Leave the embankment just beyond,

Share Marsh, Carlton Colville

dropping to a bridge **C**.

Follow a grass track across the marshes for a mile (1.6km), eventually winding to a junction **D**. The path opposite enters the conservation area around Sprat's Water, rejoining the main route a little farther on. *However, those with dogs must turn left.* Carry on past a bridge, over which the reserve path emerges, and through a couple of gates to a fork. The surfaced path to the right winds beside a final length of ditch, returning you to the start point.

Pakenham Mills from Ixworth

Start	Ixworth		GPS waypoints
Distance	5 miles (8km)		TL 931 703
Approximate time	2 hours		**A** TL 931 706
Parking	Car park opposite the church		**B** TL 914 707
Refreshments	Pub at Ixworth		**C** TL 911 702
Ordnance Survey maps	Landranger 155 (Bury St Edmunds), Explorers 211 (Bury St Edmunds & Stowmarket) and 229 (Thetford Forest in The Brecks)		**D** TL 937 688

This short and easy route uses bridleways and quiet lanes around Ixworth in mid-Suffolk. It takes in the lovely windmill and watermill belonging to the neighbouring parish of Pakenham before returning to the village whose attractive High Street has old inns and houses.

The village hall car park is opposite the church at the southern end of Ixworth. Turn right from the car park and then left opposite The Pykkerell Inn, down Commister Lane. Around a bend, take the bridleway on the left

Pakenham Watermill

almost opposite Abbey Close **A**, which runs on a causeway past the grounds of Ixworth Abbey.

The house takes its name from the Augustinian priory that was built on the site in 1170. The present house incorporates much of the fabric of the monastery, including a Norman undercroft. The ditches on either side of the causeway were probably monks' fish ponds.

Cross the River Black Bourn at Hempyard Bridge and keep ahead on a field track towards a small wood. It bends right in front of the trees, later running beside a hedge. At the end of a hedgerow go left **B** onto a grass track. Bear left again at the next corner across the ditch and follow it past a clump of trees, where the lack of a hedgerow opens a panoramic vista.

Turn left when faced by a metal gate **C** along a farm track, Heath Lane. Beyond Gameclose Covert, views open up to Ixworth, whilst on the low hill in front, Pakenham windmill comes into sight. Keep ahead to the main A143 and continue up the hill along Cutter's Lane opposite. There was a sizeable Roman fort at Ixworth that covered seven acres (2.8ha) and the lane across the top follows the line of a Roman road, which ran past it to The Wash.

Carry on along Thieves Lane beside the black-tarred Pakenham windmill, which is five storeys high and was built in 1816. It is still fully operational and can be viewed at certain times; enquire at the farm. The lane drops to Fulmer Bridge where there is a scene of meadows and stream that recalls works by the artists Constable or Cotman. Now called Broadway, the lane continues to a T-junction **D**. Go left and then shortly, left again, winding through the hamlet past a tiny Methodist chapel to the beautiful Pakenham watermill. There has been a mill on the site since at least the year 1086 and, like the windmill seen earlier, this 18th-century mill has been restored to working order. It is open to the public on Thursdays and weekends during the summer.

Mickle Mere, a small wetland nature reserve, can be seen to the right as the lane then approaches the main road. Turn left along the pavement, crossing after 50 yds (46m) at a white post to a byway on the other side. Follow it left and then right at Mill Road West to return to the starting point opposite Ixworth church.

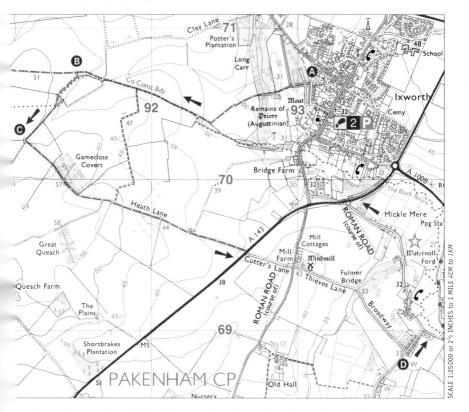

Southwold

		GPS waypoints
Start	Southwold pier	🖉 TM 511 767
Distance	3¾ miles (6km)	Ⓐ TM 512 769
Approximate time	1½ hours	Ⓑ TM 504 768
Parking	Car park to north of pier	Ⓒ TM 494 758
Refreshments	Pub at Southwold harbour, pubs and cafés in town	Ⓓ TM 501 750
Ordnance Survey maps	Landranger 156 (Saxmundham), Explorer 231 (Southwold & Bungay)	

Southwold's character stems chiefly from the diverse architecture of its seafront. This walk around its island shows that it has far more to offer — a river busy with fishing and pleasure craft and lonely marshes beautiful beneath a wide East Anglian sky.

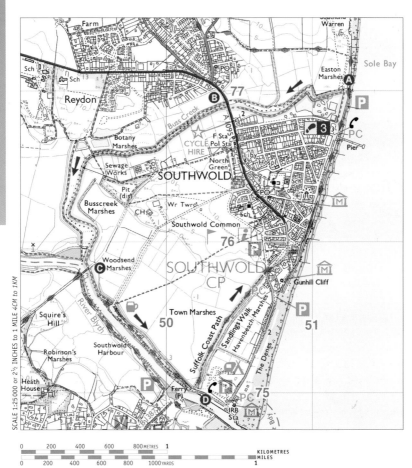

SCALE 1:25000 or 2½ INCHES to 1 MILE 4CM to 1KM

0	200	400	600	800 METRES	1		
						KILOMETRES	
						MILES	
0	200	400	600	800	1000 YARDS		1

Southwold beach

📝 Walk northwards from the pier past a row of colourful beach huts beside the car park. Turn left just before the top end of the car park Ⓐ onto a footpath that heads past the boating lake and across the marshes.

To the left the lake is a haven for waterfowl, especially in winter when visiting geese dispute territory with resident species. Behind, the town presents a fine picture with the light-house and church breaking the skyline, a different aspect to that normally seen from the greens or seafront.

Cross the road beside Might's Bridge Ⓑ and take the footpath on the south side of Buss Creek to continue around the circumference of the island. The creek is a popular venue with anglers, and its meandering course provides pleasant walking. Keep ahead past a bridge as another footpath crosses, the way developing a wonderful air of remoteness as apparent signs of habitation become more distant. Farther on the banktop path swings around, giving another view of Southwold in which the water tower, so deplored by the art historian Pevsner, is prominent.

Within a short distance the path turns southwards, passing the debouchement of the creek where it falls into the River Blyth. Just beyond, the piers that once carried the railway line now support a footbridge Ⓒ. Do not cross but keep ahead on the riverbank beside a long line of moorings, eventually reaching The Harbour Inn. A marker on the wall shows that floods can wreak havoc here, but the inn survives and has served generations of seafarers as well as the more recent tourists.

The rough road through the harbour continues past boatyards, chandlers, fish shops and idiosyncratic fishermen's huts. When all these end, turn left just before a caravan site onto a path beneath a flood bank Ⓓ. This passes through thorn thicket and then runs on at the edge of the marsh, giving a fine prospect of the town in which the church, lighthouse and Adnams brewery can all be seen. The path joins a track coming off the marshes. Keep ahead when this meets a road at the edge of South Green, a delightful open space surrounded by elegant buildings.

Turn right at a postbox to walk beside Acton Lodge to the seafront and go left along the promenade to return to the pier. Southwold is one of the country's most attractive seaside resorts, with a row of splendid buildings overlooking the sea that date mainly from Regency and early Victorian times when the town became fashionable. Beyond St James Green are the lighthouse, Sole Bay Inn and the brewery, but the line of old hotels is broken as several were destroyed during the Second World War.

Darmsden and the Gipping valley

Darmsden and the Gipping valley

		GPS waypoints	
Start	Needham Lake, Needham Market	...	TM 093 546
Distance	4¼ miles (6.8km)	**A**	TM 090 549
Approximate time	2 hours	**B**	TM 091 543
Parking	Car park at start	**C**	TM 090 533
Refreshments	Pubs and cafés at Needham Market	**D**	TM 100 533
		E	TM 106 536
Ordnance Survey maps	Landranger 155 (Bury St Edmunds), Explorer 211 (Bury St Edmunds & Stowmarket)		

The towpath between Stowmarket and Ipswich following the River Gipping, a commercial waterway in the 19th century, makes an excellent linear walk. This circular route takes in upland scenery and a lovely hamlet overlooking the valley as well as the beautiful towpath.

There are two car parks at Needham Lake and if you park in the one on the eastern side you will have to cross the footbridge to reach the one nearest the main road, where there are public toilets. Walk beside the lake past the rangers' office, continuing below

Swans on the River Gipping

the railway embankment at the edge of open meadow. Reaching a waypost **A**, turn left and duck your head to pass through a low tunnel beneath the railway, emerging beside the Victorian station. Keep ahead through Station Yard to the High Street opposite The Swan Inn. Go left along Ipswich Road, leaving right up Grinsted Hill when you reach The Lion Inn. After 100 yds (91m) turn left onto a footpath waymarked 'Barking and Back Again' **B**.

The path is enclosed as it climbs past chalk quarries on the left. Carry on at the top of the hill as it emerges into fields, where Darmsden chapel is an obvious landmark ahead. Bear right when the track divides, staying with it as it bends right to

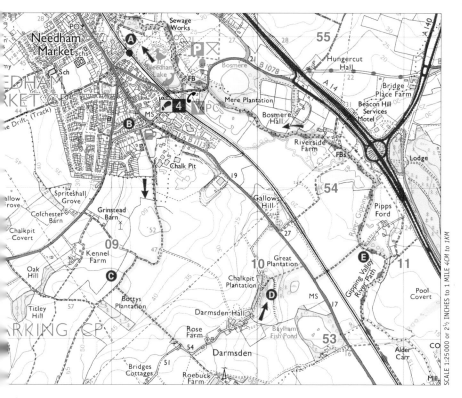

SCALE 1:25000 or 2½ INCHES to 1 MILE 4CM to 1KM

0	200	400	600	800 METRES	1
					KILOMETRES
					MILES
0	200	400	600 YARDS	½	

reach a junction of paths. Turn left and, when you reach a gravel track, go left again **C**, rising beyond a dip to the chapel. It is a lovely little building and still in use even though there is no electricity. It dates from 1888 and served about 70 souls when it was built, but just a handful attend today.

Keep ahead as you join a lane just beyond the chapel, shortly bearing left at a junction to walk past cottages and Darmsden Hall. There is then a view right to Shrubland Hall, a spectacular Italianate mansion remodelled by Sir Charles Barry between 1848 and 1852. Entering Chalkpit Plantation, look for a waymarked path on the right **D** that descends through the trees. Continue at the edge of the wood and then across a field to meet the main road by a rusting tin hut. Turn right for 100 yds (91m)

before going left over a stile beside a gate at the entrance to a landfill site. Where the track bends left, keep ahead to cross the railway line and carry on over open ground to reach the River Gipping at Pipps Ford Lock **E**.

Turn left along the bank, an excellent habitat for a wide variety of birdlife. In winter the bordering meadows are often flooded but it is unusual to find the path impassable. Footbridges take the route across a loop of the river created to serve a watermill that has long since gone. There is another former lock at Riverside Farm, beyond which is a particularly pretty stretch that runs beneath poplars. Passing a fishing lake, a grass track develops that leads to the road by a converted watermill. Turning right, cross both the road and the river, dropping into a field beside it. Walk up past the mill and Bosmere Lock to the eastern car park, re-crossing the river back to the start. ●

Dingle Marshes from Dunwich

		GPS waypoints	
Start	Dunwich beach	🥾	TM 478 706
Distance	4¼ miles (6.8km)	Ⓐ	TM 488 729
Approximate time	2½ hours	Ⓑ	TM 486 732
Parking	Car park at start	Ⓒ	TM 482 729
Refreshments	Pub, café and tearoom at Dunwich	Ⓓ	TM 473 707
Ordnance Survey maps	Landranger 156 (Saxmundham), Explorer 231 (Southwold & Bungay)		

Dunwich is the Avalon of Suffolk. Stand on the beach on a still, moonlit night and you may well think that you can hear the bells of its six churches that lie beneath the waves. Certainly Dunwich has a romance all its own, with marshes, forest and lonely shore all to be seen on this short walk.

Dunwich, a bustling town in Anglo-Saxon times and, until the 14th century a thriving seaport, suffered its demise long before global warming became a fact of life. Its decline took place in a matter of 100 years, when a series of violent storms wrought havoc, not only blocking off the harbour but also eroding the shoreline to such an extent that the large town virtually vanished. The last of its six medieval churches slipped down the cliff in 1904 and now only the ruin of the Franciscan priory reflects the splendour that once was Dunwich, even that having been rebuilt in 1289 after the initial foundation had become threatened by the waves.

The shoreline at Dunwich

🥾 Head northwards along the

shore. Initially there is a grassy path behind the shingle bank that makes good walking. However, once this reaches the reedy lagoons, you must climb onto the embankment and continue along that. Anyone with an interest in ornithology will have his binoculars at the ready as the pools attract a wide range of native and migrating birds. The landmarks of Southwold – lighthouse, church and brewery – become more distinct as you progress northwards.

After nearly 1½ miles (2.4km) by the sea, Great Dingle Farm can be seen nestling in a clump of trees behind the marsh. Drop off the shingle to a path beginning beside an English Nature noticeboard **A**. It follows the top of a low causeway that snakes across the marshes past reed-filled lagoons, making vaguely towards the ruin of a drainage mill and the distant tower of Walberswick church. Reaching a junction beside a yellow-topped marker post and small information panel **B**, go left. The path skirts a small, nameless promontory, ultimately leaving the marshes through a gate. The onward route, indicated by occasional wayposts, passes through rough grazing around the lonely outpost of Great Dingle Farm to join a track leading into woodland **C**.

Beyond the pinewood of Sandymount Covert, the higher ground gives wide views across the marshes to the shoreline. Meeting more forest by

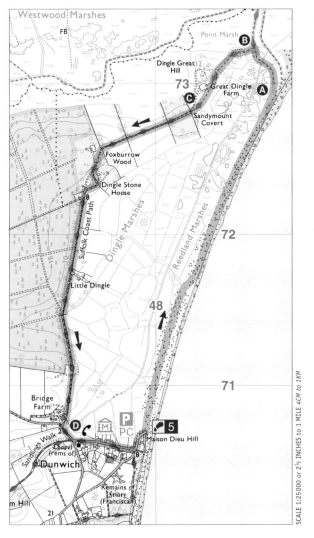

Dingle Stone House the sandy track runs on beside it, eventually winding past Bridge Farm, where there is a tearoom, to end at the lane **D**.

Turn left onto the road and then fork left at the Victorian church. St James was built beside the ruin of a medieval leper hospital to replace All Saints, which was already threatened by the sea. Continue past the interesting museum and the pub to return to the car park at the starting point. ●

Shingle Street and Alderton

Shingle Street and Alderton

Start	Coastguard cottages, Shingle Street	GPS waypoints
Distance	4½ miles (7.2km)	 TM 369 431
Approximate time	2½ hours	Ⓐ TM 366 425
Parking	Car park at start	Ⓑ TM 363 424
Refreshments	Pub at Alderton	Ⓒ TM 360 416
		Ⓓ TM 356 416
		Ⓔ TM 345 423
Ordnance Survey maps	Landranger 169 (Ipswich & The Naze), Explorer 197 (Ipswich, Felixstowe & Harwich)	

Shingle Street is just that, a lonely row of houses and cottages behind a beach of small stones, which in spring becomes a nesting site for ringed plovers and little terns. The short walk takes in the pleasant village of Alderton as well as two of the Martello towers built between 1810 and 1812 to guard the coast against French invasion.

Park before the coastguard cottages, walk past an information board to the beach and turn right to head southwards along the shore.

The sea has graded the pebbles so that the smaller ones are nearer the sea. The shingle supports several rare plants right up to the tideline, including the sea pea (*Lathyrus japonicus*) and yellow horned poppy (*Glaucium flavum*). Little terns fly here from Africa in the spring to nest, so in this season it is best to walk below the tideline and keep dogs on the lead.

Martello towers built as defence against Napoleonic invasion

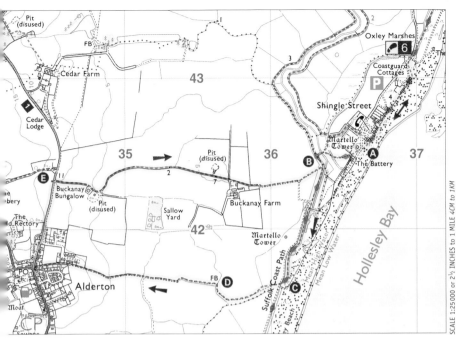

SCALE 1:25000 or 2½ INCHES to 1 MILE 4CM to 1KM

Beyond the cottages, leave the beach for a fenced path beside the Martello tower **Ⓐ**. These copied the design of a coastal tower seen by Royal Engineers at Martella in Corsica in 1794, and were part of countrywide coastal defences against a threatened Napoleonic invasion. Most of those surviving have been converted into residences or holiday homes.

Bear left on a beaten path across the grazing marsh to a point on the flood bank where it is crossed by telephone lines **Ⓑ**. Second World War defences are to be seen on the marshes to the left in the form of pillboxes and concrete tank traps, whilst offshore container ships often lie waiting for high tide to take them into Felixstowe. Walk left along the bank, passing another Martello tower, this one deserted and topped by a wartime machine gun emplacement.

A third Martello tower lies ahead, but about halfway between the two, mount a stile **Ⓒ** and drop right off the embankment to a track. Cross and walk away on a field track, shortly going over a ditch to swing beside it. Ignore

the first bridge that you come to at the field corner, continuing to a second one a little farther on **Ⓓ**. A path heads left between the fields towards houses grouped around a low hill. Later meeting a track, wind left and right to climb on with the hedge on your right. Leaving at the top, walk behind houses and a playing field before emerging in Alderton. *If you wish to stop for refreshment, the village inn, The Swan, is a few steps to the left, otherwise continue the walk by turning right up Hollesley Road.*

After ½ mile (800m) turn right **Ⓔ** to follow a farm lane signed to Buckanay Farm. Keep with the tarmac past a cottage and then later, the farm buildings. Where it subsequently swings right, go ahead across a narrow field and a drainage ditch to regain the flood wall **Ⓑ**. Retrace your steps across the grazing and past the Martello tower, returning to the coastguard cottages, either on the beach or along the road. ●

Covehithe and Benacre

		GPS waypoints
Start	Covehithe	
Distance	5½ miles (8.9km)	🖈 TM 521 818
Approximate time	2½ hours	Ⓐ TM 523 809
		Ⓑ TM 533 838
Parking	Along the lane towards Southwold from junction near church	Ⓒ TM 518 841
		Ⓓ TM 512 831
Refreshments	None	Ⓔ TM 512 822
Ordnance Survey maps	Landranger 156 (Saxmundham), Explorer 231 (Southwold & Bungay)	

The delightful shoreline part of the route has a desert island feel to it as it passes the lagoon-like Benacre Broad, but may not be passable at exceptional tides. Elsewhere the walking is easy on quiet lanes and a woodland track. As the route passes through a Suffolk Wildlife Trust Reserve, dogs should be kept on the lead.

In its prime Covehithe was a busy port, hence the erstwhile magnificence of its church which would have rivalled that of Blythburgh. Although Cromwell has been blamed for its ruinous state, it appears that the small thatched church built within the shell of the nave in 1672 reflects the decline of Covehithe after its medieval prosperity rather than the result of Puritan vandalism.

🖈 From the junction, walk towards the church, turning right almost

Covehithe cliffs

immediately onto a path to Covehithe Beach. Meeting a farm track, go right, soon branching off right again onto a well-trodden path that leads to the shore by Covehithe Broad Ⓐ. Turn north along the beach *below the crumbling cliffs, which are receding faster than any others in the country and should therefore be given a wide berth to avoid falling debris.* In ½ mile (800m), look for a telegraph cable dangling uselessly from the bank, which marks the truncated lane that once ran to the harbour.

Approaching Benacre Broad, the skeletal remains of trees scatter the beach, uprooted as the cliffs on which they perched were undercut by the waves. The area is part of a National Nature Reserve and includes a diverse range of habitats encompassing beach, dunes, heath, broads and woodland.

Beyond the lake, you can either climb to a path above or remain on the beach. Walk for another ½ mile (800m) to the end of the cliffs, where a concrete track heads inland **B**. During the Second World War this part of the coastline was vulnerable to invasion and the concrete track was laid to link the defence works put in place. Scattered about, half-hidden by the sand, are pillboxes and tank traps and the lagoon just to the north was one of three gravel pits from which the ballast to build them was dug, the other two having been engulfed by the sea. Overgrowth soon narrows the broad way to an attractive path, leading to the entrance of the thatched Beach Farm. Again on a track, carry on ahead towards the tower of Benacre church, almost hidden by trees in summer.

Reaching a lane **C**, go left. It rarely sees much traffic and twists and turns for ³/₄ mile (1.2km) to reach a sharp right-hand bend by a clump of old oak and lime trees **D**. Leave through a gate on the left along a track signed as a byway, shortly curving at the perimeter of a meadow fringing Holly Hang woodland. Carry on at the edge of another wood, Holly Grove, to emerge onto a lane at the far side **E**. Go left and walk the pleasant ¹/₂ mile (800m) back to the starting point. ●

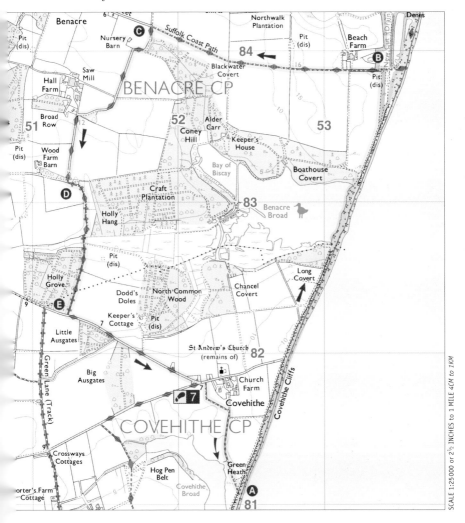

Nowton Park and High Suffolk

Start	Nowton Park, Bury St Edmunds (to south of town)	GPS waypoints
Distance	4½ miles (7.2km)	🔍 TL 864 621
Approximate time	2 hours	Ⓐ TL 861 622
Parking	Car park at start	Ⓑ TL 860 615
Refreshments	At the Ranger Centre at weekends and in school holidays	Ⓒ TL 851 613
		Ⓓ TL 858 605
		Ⓔ TL 865 607
Ordnance Survey maps	Landranger 155 (Bury St Edmunds), Explorer 211 (Bury St Edmunds & Stowmarket)	Ⓕ TL 865 612

This delightful ramble follows the Bury to Clare Walk onto High Suffolk, a tract of elevated land south of Bury. After visiting an isolated church, the way returns through the 200-acre (81ha) Nowton Park.

Before its acquisition by Bury Corporation in 1985, Nowton Court and park belonged to the Oakes family. A banker and County Treasurer, Oakes built a 'large and handsome mansion' and planted the famous Lime Avenue as well as an arboretum containing both native species and specimen trees from around the world.

🔍 Walk to the end of the car park farthest from the Ranger Centre and toilets, where there is a noticeboard marking the start of the Bury to Clare Walk, a meandering route of around 18½ miles (29km) amongst some of the finest scenery of 'High Suffolk'. Follow the path through trees to the road and go right. Opposite Plovers' Way, abandon it for a bridleway on the left signed to Breckey Ley. Carry on past the entrance to the house, swinging left where the way splits at the corner of the grounds Ⓐ. Remain beside the wood at the edge of open country, meeting a lane at the end. Follow it ahead for

some 550 yds (503m) before leaving right Ⓑ onto an inviting bridleway.

Rising gently between the fields, there is a glimpse left to Nowton church, hardly seen again until you reach it later. Near the summit of the hill is a crossing of paths Ⓒ. Go left and, in the field corner by a stand of trees, cross a ditch to continue on its opposite flank past a triangulation pillar, eventually meeting Park Lane.

Now parting company with the Bury to Clare Walk, follow the lane left, a quiet, broad-verged byway that allows views over a wide tract of countryside. Behind Bury stands a large sugar beet factory, a long plume of white smoke often emanating from its chimney. When the lane bends sharply left by a thatched cottage, keep ahead on a gravel track. After 20 yds (18m), leave over a stile on the left Ⓓ and strike a diagonal across a meadow, where decaying oak trees show it once to have been parkland belonging to Nowton

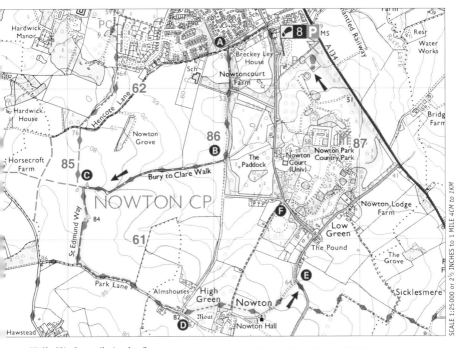

Hall. Climb a stile in the far corner to walk through a paddock behind a barn. Cross a farm drive and then another meadow before reaching St Peter's Church, hidden behind trees until the last moment. The small Norman church was founded for monks from St Edmund's Abbey who worked in vineyards on these rolling hills; the chancel was added early in the 14th century. After the Dissolution, the church remained in use by the villagers and was restored in 1843.

In Nowton Park

Follow the lane left to a road **E** and go left again into the hamlet. Keep left when the road later bends in front of a junction. Just after the pavement ends, look for a gate on the right into Nowton Park **F**. Disregarding the 'Private' sign, go through to a waymarked path. Several walks lead to the park's many features: an arboretum, a maze, wildflower meadows, ponds and a bird hide. One of the showpieces is Lime Avenue, which in spring is ablaze with countless daffodils. *The quickest way back is along the waymarked circular walk to the left, which ultimately returns you to the Ranger Centre along Lime Avenue. But to see more of the park, instead follow the waymarks right, winding around the arboretum and alternating beyond between open meadow and woodland. Eventually, approaching playing fields, you can bear left across the park or stay with the wooded perimeter, either way returning to the car park.* ●

Forest and riverside from West Stow

		GPS waypoints
Start	Forest Lodge Picnic Site, West Stow	
		✏ TL 815 714
Distance	5¼ miles (8.4km)	Ⓐ TL 814 718
		Ⓑ TL 828 721
Approximate time	2½ hours	Ⓒ TL 837 720
Parking	Car park at start	Ⓓ TL 831 712
Refreshments	None en route	Ⓔ TL 821 705
Ordnance Survey maps	Landranger 144 (Thetford & Diss), Explorer 229 (Thetford Forest in The Brecks)	Ⓕ TL 816 703

This short walk in the Breckland of north Suffolk displays a wide variety of scenery: forest, farmland and the parkland surrounding Culford School, closing with a short length along the footpath beside the northern bank of the River Lark.

West Stow lies on the fringe of the East Anglian Brecklands, a large area cleared for agriculture during the Stone Age, but abandoned to grazing after the sandy soils lost their fertility. The present forests date from the early 20th century, when large areas of poor land were put to forest.

✏ From the car park entrance turn left past black wooden huts. Follow a sandy forest track for 300 yds (274m) to a junction Ⓐ. Turn off right onto a narrower path threading through the fringe of the forest with open fields to the right. When the path later swings left, keep ahead out of the trees, negotiating a barbed wire barrier designed to keep stock in the fields rather than people out. Continue forward on a farm track through a meadow towards tiny Wordwell church. Passing into another field, the track curves left in front of the pink-washed Wordwell Hall. Follow the drive right to a lane Ⓑ.

Cross to the track opposite and head straight out over the fields to Blake's Spinney. Pass through the trees and continue beyond at the field edge to a junction with the Icknield Way Path Ⓒ. This long-distance trail follows the line of a prehistoric trackway that pre-dates the Peddars Way and runs down the chalky spine of southern England from the north Norfolk coast to Avebury on the Wiltshire downs.

Turn right, the dead straight track eventually emerging onto a lane at Brockley Corner. Go right for about ¹⁄₃ mile (536m) to find a waymarked farm track leaving on the left Ⓓ. It leads past a water tower and then through a wood, breaking out onto the edge of Culford School playing fields. A waymark directs you across on a left diagonal, passing behind a couple of annexe buildings to meet a junction of drives. Turn right to walk in front of the original hall, continuing along a gravel track past a cricket field, a graceful iron bridge and then an ornamental lake.

The lake at Culford

Just before reaching the end of the lake, fork off right on a waymarked path **E** that leads out to a lane opposite West Stow church. Go left, shortly taking the first right towards Flempton and walking down as far as a bridge over the River Lark **F**.

Leave right immediately before it onto the Lark Valley Path, a 13-mile (20.9km) route that follows the course of the River Lark from Mildenhall to Bury St Edmunds. This section is a birdwatcher's delight for it runs along a raised bank between the river and flooded pools. Reedbeds and overhanging willows provide nesting cover for waterbirds and there is always the chance of spotting a heron or even a kingfisher.

After crossing the Culford Culvert, a broader path develops that ushers you away from the river. Bend right in front of a clump of oak and then curve left beside a plantation of pine, before long passing behind foresters' cottages to reach a lane at the edge of West Stow. Go right, but in a few yards take the first turning on the left, a broad track that leads back to the starting point at the Forest Lodge Picnic Site. ●

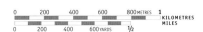

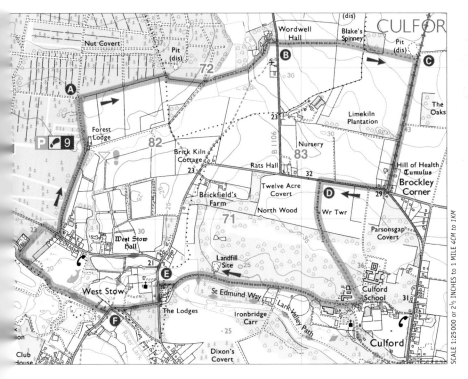

Eye and Braiseworth

Eye and Braiseworth

			GPS waypoints	
Start	Eye		📍	TM 145 738
Distance	5 miles (8km). Shorter version		Ⓐ	TM 151 738
	2½ miles (4km)		Ⓑ	TM 152 736
Approximate time	2 hours		Ⓒ	TM 146 728
Parking	Buckshorn Lane car park		Ⓓ	TM 140 710
Refreshments	Pub and tearoom at Eye		Ⓔ	TM 135 713
Ordnance Survey maps	Landrangers 144 (Thetford & Diss)		Ⓕ	TM 140 721
	and 156 (Saxmundham),		Ⓖ	TM 143 730
	Explorer 230 (Diss & Harleston)			

Eye, stranded away from main roads, is a charming town, the tower of its church justly described as one of the wonders of Suffolk. The heart of the town contains many interesting old buildings, including the timber-framed guildhall, all overlooked by the scanty remains of a castle, to which there is a path signed from the car park. The surrounding countryside is attractive with the diminutive River Dove having its source close to the town.

📍 Turn left out of the car park by the library and walk to the end of Buckshorn Lane, passing a succession of pleasant cottages. Go left again below Castle Hill to reach the church.

No visitor to Eye should leave the town without seeing the church. Though the 101-ft (31m) tower is its most spectacular and lavish feature, the interior is hardly less impressive, with a beautifully restored rood screen on which painted panels depict saints and kings. The early 16th-century half-timbered guildhall stands close to the church, its woodwork richly ornamented with carvings.

Follow the main road past the south side of the church and cross the lovely River Dove by Abbey Bridge. The name refers to the Benedictine monastery that once stood on the east bank of the river. The fish ponds survive but little else. Immediately after the bridge turn right Ⓐ along Ludgate Causeway, following

a sign to The Pennings, a picnic area and riverside nature reserve. Pass it and continue down the winding lane. After a left bend and a garden wall adorned with ornamental lions, turn off right onto a drive, crossing a stile by a gate into the field behind Ⓑ.

Waymarked the Mid Suffolk Footpath, it runs at the edge of consecutive rough meadows to end at the B1077 beside 'Big Head', part of the Oak Sculpture Trail. Cross to Park Lane on the other side, a pleasant country track lined with sapling oaks, given in 1998 by a variety of local organisations to replace a lost hedgerow. It leads past a succession of reed-filled ponds, *shortly passing a path off on the right, which offers a short cut back to the village* Ⓒ. The route, however, continues along the track, bearing left at a fork to rise gently onto the higher ground at the edge of the valley. Keep going as it later swings right, shortly

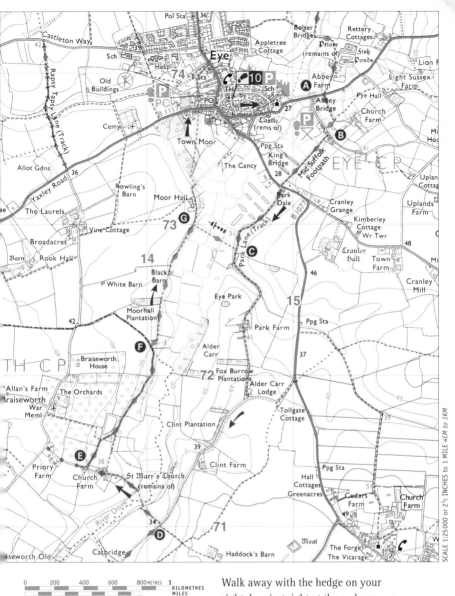

SCALE 1:25000 or 2½ INCHES to 1 MILE 4CM to 1KM

reaching Park Farm. Walk past the farmhouse and through the farmyard, leaving along a concrete track that ends between a pair of lodges at a lane.

Turn right and walk along the road for almost ¾ mile (1.2km), taking in the fine views to the right and passing Clint Farm on the left. After going beneath power lines and around a gentle curve, look for a path leaving on the right beside a hedge separating the fields **D**.

Walk away with the hedge on your right, bearing right at the end across a narrow field to a footbridge spanning the River Dove. Keep on over another meadow to a stile beginning a tunnel-hedged path.

This enclosed way was once the path to St Mary's Church at Braiseworth, only the chancel of which survives. A Victorian church was built to replace it nearer to the centre of the tiny village, which incorporated the old church's best feature, an elaborately carved doorway. Walk past the church and through the yard of Church Farm to leave along its access track. Just beyond the gate and almost opposite the abandoned Priory Cottage, turn right  **E** onto a bridleway. It is known locally as Fen Lane, for it skirts the watermeadows bordering the river.

The bridleway runs as a pleasant old track through a long line of thicket below a succession of orchards. Follow it for a little over $^1/_2$ mile (800m) then look for a waymark taking the Mid Suffolk Footpath over a stile on the right **F**. Cross the small field diagonally to a redundant stile and, entering the next meadow, go left staying close to the fence. As you head back towards Eye, there are glimpses of the distant town hall clock tower and church breaking the skyline behind the trees. Beyond a stile and plank bridge at the end of a belt of trees, keep ahead along a short boundary that sets your direction across a large field towards the low remains of Black Barn at the far side.

Climb a stile by the ruin and walk on beside successive meadows, keeping a hedgerow on your left. *The short cut path from Park Lane later joins from the right by a large oak tree* **G**.

Carry on, eventually leaving the fields over a stile by Moor Hall Farm to join its driveway. After 50 yds (46m) the drive bends right. Pass through an opening on the left waymarked as a circular walk, following a ditch to a concrete bridge into woodland.

Victorian town hall in Eye

Immediately within the fringe of the wood, fork right, passing a pond and before long crossing another footbridge. A little farther on go right out of the wood over a final bridge. Bear left across a recreation ground, exiting beside the community hall and changing rooms. Cross a road and walk through the old station yard, now used by a variety of light industries, keeping to the right to find a grassy path running at the edge of more woodland. Reaching the road almost opposite a row of quaint almshouses, turn right and walk up to the Victorian town hall. Just beyond, go left into Church Street and then right into Buckshorn Lane to return to the starting point. ●

Constable Country — Flatford and East Bergholt

		GPS waypoints
Start	East Bergholt	TM 069 346
Distance	5½ miles (8.9km)	Ⓐ TM 060 346
Approximate time	2½ hours	Ⓑ TM 060 343
Parking	Car park at village centre	Ⓒ TM 068 339
Refreshments	Pubs in East Bergholt and tea garden at Flatford	Ⓓ TM 067 336
		Ⓔ TM 077 331
Ordnance Survey maps	Landrangers 168 (Colchester) and 169 (Ipswich & The Naze), Explorer 196 (Sudbury, Hadleigh & Dedham Vale)	Ⓕ TM 081 331
		Ⓖ TM 088 333
		Ⓗ TM 086 341
		Ⓙ TM 072 338

John Constable, the best-known painter of the English landscape, grew up in the lovely surroundings of the Stour valley, which forms the boundary between Suffolk and Essex. Although Constable died more than 150 years ago, much of the countryside he captured on canvas survives almost unaltered and is instantly recognisable.

Go right out of the car park past The Red Lion and turn right into the lane by the post office. Constable's early studio is the building on the other side of the road and belongs to the East Bergholt Society, who purchased it in 1802, 35 years before the artist's death. Pass the Congregational church and a cemetery and then, reaching a gate into Vale Farm, follow a contained path to its left, which descends to a stream and drive by a cottage. Cross and take the path climbing through a pasture on the other side. A classic view of Dedham Vale is revealed at the top, one that appeared in several of Constable's works. To the left is Dedham itself, the great tower of its church the dominating feature. Ahead is Stratford St Mary and its smaller church with the A12 beyond, a modern addition that, from here at least, hardly mars the scene.

Turn left at a footpath junction Ⓐ along a delightful sunken path. Go left again at the bottom Ⓑ onto a hedged path, which in places has more the characteristic of a wood. Reaching a green track at the end, swing right and then, in front of a gate, left, re-crossing the stream that you encountered back at Vale Farm to enter Fishpond Wood. Ignore the immediate stile and walk on a few yards within the fringe to another stile. Keep going with a hedge on your right along the lower edge of a field, crossing at the corner to continue with it now on your left. Farther on, the path becomes contained, emerging at the far end into a willow-fringed meadow. Bear left along its perimeter, leaving over a stile in the corner onto a track Ⓒ.

Follow it right, taking the right branch signed to Flatford when it divides, to cross a tributary stream. At

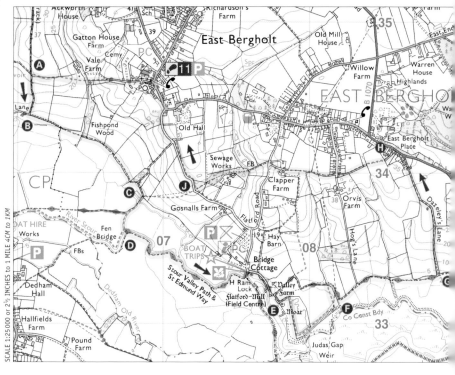

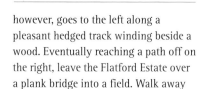

the next fork bear left, the footpath leading to a footbridge across the River Stour **D**. Turn left along the riverbank. This part of the route is magnificent and one of the finest riverside walks in Suffolk. All sorts of wildlife may be seen as you wander beside the water, including herons and perhaps even a kingfisher.

At length, reaching a footbridge, cross the river and walk up beside the pretty 16th-century Bridge Cottage, which houses an exhibition on Constable. Go right to pass Flatford Mill, now a field centre but once owned by Constable's father, and then Willy Lott's House, both so famously depicted in his paintings.

Bear left to pass the field centre's car park but then go right **E** onto a National Trust permissive path that takes you round the bank of a delightful pond, the habitat of a wide variety of water birds and geese. At the far end of the pond, there is a bird hide to the right overlooking the water. The route,

however, goes to the left along a pleasant hedged track winding beside a wood. Eventually reaching a path off on the right, leave the Flatford Estate over a plank bridge into a field. Walk away by the right-hand boundary, passing beneath power cables to a stile in the corner **F**.

Turn left to follow a hedgerow at the edge of a succession of meadows that are likely to be damp in winter. Ignore an opening on the left, the end of Hog's Lane, and keep going until you eventually reach a large wooden cattle pen. Leave the watermeadows through a gate immediately before it **G**, climbing away along a stony track, Dazeley's Lane. Reaching a road at the top walk left, but abandon it after 50 yds (46m), turning left again at the end of Clarence Villas **H** down a narrow enclosed path. Strike across a field, passing through a small thicket at the far side to another length of contained path.

Cross a track, Hog's Lane, to a footpath on the other side, following the field edge to Clapper Farm. Leave along its drive, but just before its end, the right of way cuts right over a stile and across the foot of a paddock to meet the lane from the neighbouring driveway. Opposite, the ongoing footpath falls gently beside a field to cross a stream and enter a wood. Bear left at a fork, emerging onto a grass track. Keep ahead across a final small paddock to reach another lane **J**. Go right, initially avoiding the tarmac by using a parallel path along the bank. Continue up the lane after the two come together to a junction in front of East Bergholt church. This is worth a visit, if only to see the unique timber Bell House in the churchyard. Built after the construction of the enormous west tower was abandoned in 1525, it houses a full set of bells, which are swung by hand cranks rather than the traditional bell-ropes. Turn left into the village, passing the site of East Bergholt House, Constable's childhood home. ●

Flatford Mill, East Bergholt

Cretingham and Brandeston

		GPS waypoints
Start	Oak Corner, Cretingham	TM 227 603
Distance	5 miles (8km)	**A** TM 227 608
Approximate time	2 hours	**B** TM 242 608
Parking	Street parking in village is limited, but walkers patronising The Bell may use its car park	**C** TM 243 611
		D TM 246 613
		E TM 251 604
Refreshments	Pubs at Cretingham and Brandeston, restaurant at Cretingham Golf Club	**F** TM 249 594
		G TM 241 595
		H TM 233 598
Ordnance Survey maps	Landranger 156 (Saxmundham), Explorer 212 (Woodbridge & Saxmundham)	

The beautiful countryside of the Deben valley around the villages of Cretingham, Brandeston, Monewden and Hoo is particularly appealing to walkers with its excellent network of footpaths and bridleways. The small villages are virtually unspoilt and several have excellent pubs.

The magnificent oak tree opposite The Bell is the starting point of the walk. Follow the village street towards Earl Soham past the post office and the church. Much of the church building dates from c 1300, but there were alterations and additions in the later Perpendicular style. The 14th-century porch leads through to an 18th-century interior, when each family was segregated within their own box pew and the priest delivered his sermon from the commanding triple-decker pulpit, crowned by a tester that echoed his voice around the nave. Above is a fine hammerbeam roof, its weight producing a decided lean in the north wall. There are several memorials to a branch of the Cornwallis family, who lived here in the early 17th century, and the finely carved medieval font still bears traces of its original paint.

Cross the little River Deben and turn right at the T-junction. After 100 yds (91m), where the road bends left, keep ahead along a driveway to Cretingham Golf Club **A**. Keep right as it splits, passing a pond before reaching the car park. Walk left in front of the clubhouse to a junction and turn right along a wooded sandy path across the course. Over a bridge pass through a wood and carry on beside fields to a lane. Turn right and then immediately left into a cul-de-sac signed as a bridleway **B**.

After the thatched Grove Farm, with its decorative plasterwork known as

Ford across the River Deben

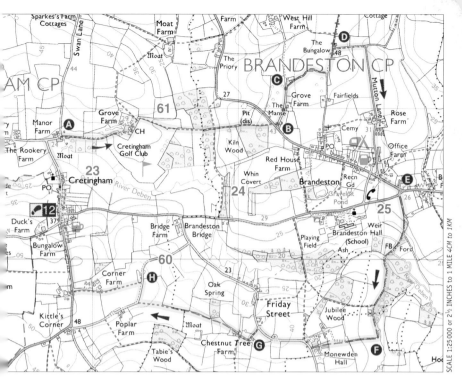

SCALE 1:25 000 or 2½ INCHES to 1 MILE 4CM to 1KM

pargeting, but before a red brick cottage, the bridleway swings off right **C** on a broad grassy track. Turn left when you reach a narrow lane and then right after 200 yds (183m) just before The Bungalow **D**. A field-edge path takes you the short distance to Mutton Lane. Go right and follow it into Brandeston by The Queen's Head pub.

Turn left to a junction with another road coming from Cretingham. Go right beside the triangular green, crossing the road to a bridleway opposite **E**. This track descends gently to the river, giving glimpses of the church and Brandeston Hall to the right. The present mock-Tudor house of 1864 replaces an Elizabethan mansion built by Andrew Revett. Since 1949 it has been the preparatory school for nearby Framlingham College.

Where the track forks, keep right and cross the footbridge to continue on the bridleway, climbing by the side of a

wood. Walk ahead through a gap at the top to join a track past an isolated farmhouse. Reaching a junction at the end of the field **F** turn right up the hill. Towards the top, near the early 18th-century Monewden Hall where the track bends sharply right, go forward across an uncultivated corner below an ash tree. Pass through a gap in a fence and across a lawn, walking out between stables to a lane. Turn right onto the lane, leaving after ¼ mile (400m) along a track on the left to Chestnut Tree Farm **G**.

Wind through the farmyard and then follow the right-hand edge of a field towards a wood. The path skirts its perimeter and continues as a field-edge path. Shortly before Poplar Farm, the hedge swings right. However, keep ahead across the last field to a lane. Turn right, but after 100 yds (91m) go left **H** onto another field-edge path. Carry on across a couple of fields to meet a lane and follow it right back into Cretingham. ●

Framlingham from Dennington

Start	Dennington church
Distance	6¼ miles (10.1km). Shorter version 5 miles (8km)
Approximate time	2½ hours
Parking	In village
Refreshments	Pub at Dennington, pubs and tearooms at Framlingham
Ordnance Survey maps	Landranger 156 (Saxmundham), Explorer 212 (Woodbridge & Saxmundham)

GPS waypoints

✎	TM 281 670
Ⓐ	TM 278 669
Ⓑ	TM 274 660
Ⓒ	TM 279 653
Ⓓ	TM 283 645
Ⓔ	TM 283 642
Ⓕ	TM 286 638
Ⓖ	TM 286 646
Ⓗ	TM 290 669

Although many hedges around Framlingham have been lost to agriculture, enough remain to guide you on this enjoyable walk between the attractive settlements of Dennington and Framlingham. A great castle and two fine churches are amongst the highlights along the way.

St Mary's Church at Dennington is famed for the craftsmanship of its medieval builders, displayed in a wealth of carving in both wood and stone. Remarkable are its richly decorated pews and a rare pyx above the altar, whilst other notable features include stained glass windows and the tomb of Sir William Phelip, who fought alongside Henry V at Agincourt.

✎ From Dennington church, follow the main A1120 for ¼ mile (400m) towards Saxtead. Where the road bends right Ⓐ, turn left into the entrance of a drive from which a signed footpath branches past a house and behind the gardens of a small property development. Continue at the edge of the fields beyond, turning the last corner to emerge over a plank bridge onto a lane. Go right and immediately right again along a concrete track, which leads past Glebe Cottage to a group of timbered buildings. Passing

them, swing right into a field and walk forward to a grass track leading left beside a ditch and subsequent hedge towards a distant wood. Where the hedge ends, cross the ditch directly in front and follow it left to a second hedge, turning right beside that to make for the wood once more. Just before reaching it, turn with the hedge to the left, a field track developing that shortly leads to a junction of tracks Ⓑ.

Walk ahead on a permissive path alongside the continuing hedge as it curves behind Dairy Farm. There is a brief view to the Gothic outlines of Framlingham College as you meander beside a wood eventually reaching a footbridge beyond the end of the trees Ⓒ. Cross and follow the River Ore left to Durrant's Bridge, there turning the field corner to find a gap onto the lane.

Rejoin the river in the field opposite and follow it away, passing ahead into a

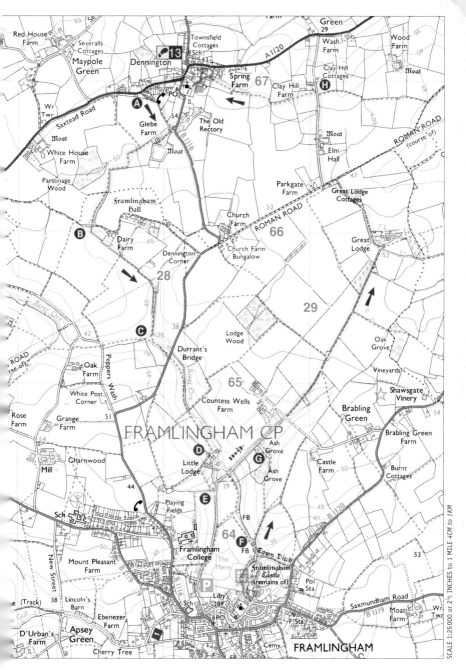

meadow at its far end. Keep going towards farm buildings and walk up to a stile in the top field corner **D**. Carry on to a footbridge and then climb beside a grass field. Turn left at the crest and as you descend alongside the hedge, Framlingham Castle comes into view. At the bottom go left again to emerge onto a narrow lane **E**.

If you do not wish to visit Framlingham, you can shorten the walk by turning left along the lane, rejoining the main route below Ash Grove **G**.

0	200	400	600	800 METRES	1
					KILOMETRES
					MILES
0	200	400	600 YARDS	½	

Framlingham Castle

Otherwise, turn right towards Framlingham. Beyond the left-hand playing field you can drop through a gate to follow a parallel path through the Mere Nature Reserve. It offers a splendid panorama across the lake to the castle, although after wet weather, the path can be muddy. Emerging beyond the reserve into a car park, wind right to rejoin the lane opposite the 17th-century Hitcham Almshouses. At the end, turn left into Bridge Street and continue up Market Hill into the town square, there turning left again into Church Street. Dedicated to St Michael, the church has a fine hammerbeam roof and several magnificent 16th and 17th-century carved tombs. Carry on past the church, but where the street then turns right, keep forward towards the castle entrance.

The remains are chiefly of the stronghold put up by the second Earl of Norfolk between 1190 and 1210, which replaced an earlier castle on the site. Its size and layout were influenced by the fortresses seen by the Crusaders on their expeditions in the Holy Land, for unlike other East Anglian castles, there is no keep dominating the outer defence works, which consist of a curtain wall with 13 towers. The gatehouse was added in the 16th century, and in the 17th century a bequest made by Sir Robert Hitcham turned the castle's great hall into a Poor House.

Just before reaching the moat bridge, go through a turnstile on the left (there is no charge) and then drop to cross the moat. Climbing to a small green below the castle walls, cross diagonally to its far corner where a stepped path descends to a bridge spanning the ancient town ditch. Walk forward through thicket to a gate, beyond which is a junction of paths **F**. Bearing slightly right of ahead, follow a rising grass path into the corner of a field and continue beside its right-hand hedge. At the crest of the rise, a gap in the hedge offers a fine retrospective view of the castle. Leave the boundary just after that point, bearing left across the field towards a copse, Ash Grove. Follow its perimeter around to the right, falling with it to a footbridge at the bottom of the field that gives onto a lane **G**.

Head right. Reaching a junction, continue ahead through gates towards Great Lodge Farm. Just before the farm, go left onto a gravel track that winds around the house and on between the wooded borders of fields. Turning left at the end, walk out past cottages to join a lane, and follow that right for $^1/_2$ mile (800m) to Clay Hill Farm **H**.

Leave through a gap on the left immediately before the farmhouse, heading across the field towards the distant tower of Dennington church. In the next field bear slightly left, but then resume your way in the third field, making for a barn. Continue past that across a rough meadow, at the far side following a contained path that skirts a recreation ground before passing behind the garden of The Queen's Head to reach the churchyard. ●

Orford coast and country

Start	Orford	**GPS waypoints**	
Distance	6¼ miles (10.1km)	🖊 TM 424 496	
Approximate time	2½ hours	Ⓐ TM 422 509	
		Ⓑ TM 428 514	
Parking	Car park on road to quay opposite Jolly Sailor inn	Ⓒ TM 428 515	
		Ⓓ TM 420 519	
Refreshments	Pubs and tearooms at Orford	Ⓔ TM 409 489	
Ordnance Survey maps	Landranger 156 (Saxmundham), Explorer 212 (Woodbridge & Saxmundham)		

Orford is a 'must' for any visitor to Suffolk, with its polygonal Norman castle and a large church that had its origins in the same age. Its importance at this time was as a port, but like so many of Suffolk's havens it began to silt up, so Defoe wrote in 1722: 'The sea daily throws up more land so it is a sea port no longer'. The walk covers field paths, lanes and the flood wall facing the River Ore, which is a popular summer walk.

🖊 Turn right out of the car park to walk up Orford's attractive main street towards the church. St Bartholomew's dates from 1166 and is contemporary with the castle, although only the ruined chancel arches remain from the original building. In the 14th century, when the place developed as a thriving seaport, the church was rebuilt and the tower added, but part of this subsequently collapsed in 1830. Amongst its treasures is a splendid font with an inscription begging prayers for the departed and also some fine brasses. In its medieval heyday Orford had two other churches plus a friary and two hospitals, their memory retained in the names of Chantry Farm and Chantry Marshes to the south.

Walk through the churchyard to avoid a dangerous corner, emerging opposite the square beside The King's Head. The castle lies beyond the far end of the square, the top of the keep giving a wonderful panorama of the country-side covered by the walk. It was built by Henry II in the 12th century to defend the coast. The route, however, continues to the right, turning right again into

The River Ore

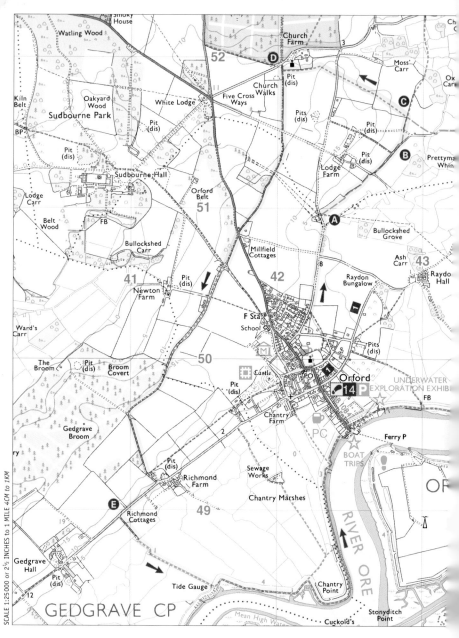

Ferry Road towards Iken. Keep ahead for ¹⁄₂ mile (800m) to reach an electricity sub-station, opposite which a bridleway is signed through the hedge **Ⓐ**. Strike out across a field, joining the left hedge at the far end. Leave through a gate in the corner and

go right and then immediately left along a field track. After some 300 yds (274m), as an isolated brick building comes into view ahead, look for a waypost **Ⓑ**.

Bear left up the banking and cut across the field to the end of a hedge. Walk on through a gate beside the hedge to another gate **Ⓒ**. Turn through it and climb upfield to a gate near the top corner. Bear right across the next field, making for a kissing-gate towards the middle of the top hedge. Cross a lane and continue on the other side, heading for the small spire of Sudbourne church, to be briefly glimpsed above trees. Joining a boundary on the right, pass the church to reach a track at the corner of the churchyard **Ⓓ**.

Turn left, shortly meeting a narrow lane. The bridleway continues opposite, after a while going through the fringe of a small wood and then crossing more fields to a road. Cross to a broad track and follow it on, passing Orford Lodge and later skirting an outpost of Tunstall Forest known as Gedgrave Broom. Eventually the main track swings to the left, ultimately ending at a lane. Go right and after almost $\frac{1}{4}$ mile (400m) turn left onto a hedged track **Ⓔ**.

It drops onto the reclaimed salt marshes, making for the distant flood bank ahead. Climb onto the wall and turn left along the top, following the sinuous course of the River Ore. This is a wonderful place to watch for oystercatchers and other waders as well as heron, who, as you approach, often wait until the last moment before lazily taking to their wings. Silence is one of the great qualities here, broken only by the call of birds and rustling of the wind. Moored craft herald the end of the path, which finally drops onto the Orford waterfront. Go left up the main street back to the car park. ●

Orford and its castle

West Row and Worlington from Mildenhall

West Row and Worlington from Mildenhall

		GPS waypoints
Start	Mildenhall	✐ TL 712 744
Distance	6¼ miles (10.1km)	Ⓐ TL 700 743
Approximate time	2½ hours	Ⓑ TL 690 743
Parking	Jubilee Hall car park	Ⓒ TL 676 746
Refreshments	Pubs at West Row, Worlington and	Ⓓ TL 691 738
	Mildenhall, cafés at Mildenhall.	Ⓔ TL 702 740
Ordnance Survey maps	Landranger 143 (Ely & Wisbech),	Ⓕ TL 713 739
	Explorer 226 (Ely & Newmarket)	

Mildenhall lies on the edge of the Fens so the fact that there are no gradients on this walk will cause little surprise. Yet the landscape has a unique appeal for many people who enjoy walking in really open country beneath vast skies. The large church in Mildenhall is worth visiting to see its beautiful stonework, executed by masons from Ely cathedral in the 13th century, and a richly decorated hammerbeam roof. Also of interest is the museum, which has a replica of a massive silver dish, part of a Roman treasure trove found in 1943.

✐ The Jubilee Hall car park is close to the centre of town. A path runs left from its entrance to the River Lark, which divides here to flow around Parker's Island. Go over the two bridges spanning the water to reach the south bank and turn right along the riverside path, soon emerging onto a road at Mill Bridge. Cross and drop back left to continue on the other bank past one of the town's former mills to Turf Lock. Beyond a footbridge, walk on by the river at the edge of a cricket ground and then a small wood.

Joining a bridleway, carry on to a cottage Ⓐ. Leave the track immediately after it in favour of a field-edge path beside the meandering Lark, where you might spot large fish basking in shaded pools. Over to the right Wamil Hall can be seen and then, after crossing a track

by a bridge, there is a pleasing view over grazing marshes to Worlington

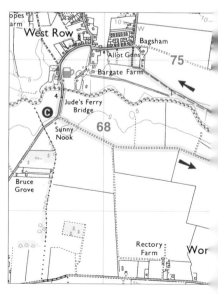

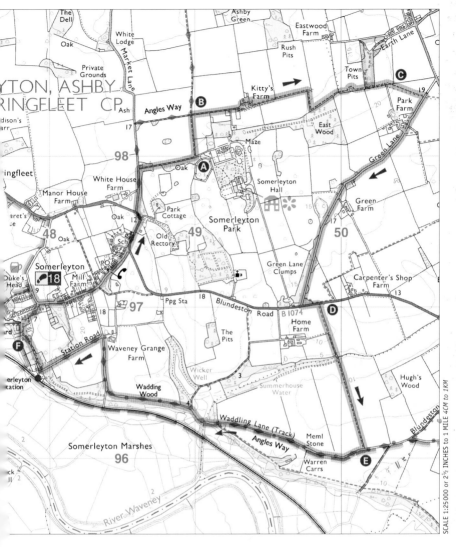

SCALE 1:25 000 or 2½ INCHES to 1 MILE 4CM to 1KM

| 0 | 200 | 400 | 600 | 800 METRES | 1 |
| 0 | 200 | 400 | 600 YARDS | ½ |

KILOMETRES
MILES

turn right onto Green Lane.

There follows a mile (1.6km) of pleasant walking along this quiet byway, from which there are glimpses to Somerleyton Hall to the right. The house is Jacobean and inside are many original features such as the fabulous plaster ceiling of the ballroom, whilst other rooms reflect the later Adam style. The exterior was remodelled in 1844 and the façade is a celebration of early Victorian Anglo-Italian style. Passing Green Farm, also notice the ancient beech trees in the wood opposite. About 50 yds (46m) before meeting the busy B1074 at the end, look for a waymarked path on the left. It winds around a clump of thicket to a gate in the park wall beyond **D**. Cross to a stile opposite and walk away at the field edge. Joining a gravel track, keep ahead over a low rise, the way eventually ending through a gate onto Waddling Lane **E**.

Suffolk was famous for its turkeys and geese and the odd name for this

Charming estate cottages in Somerleyton

beautiful green lane might well have come from the flocks of geese that were once driven along it to London's Smithfield Market, the geese wearing felt booties to protect their feet.

Turn right, passing after about ¼ mile (400m) a memorial on the right to an American aircrew who died during the war when their bomber crashed close to this spot. There are wide-reaching views across the flat valley of the River Waveney as you approach the fine pine trees that are a feature of the Somerleyton woodland.

Bear left when the way divides after dipping across a side valley and keep ahead when another track joins from the left. At the end, go left into Station Road. Leave opposite the station along a gravel track into a wood, shortly reaching an Angles Way sign **F**. Turn off left along a grass track into thicket, passing through a leylandii hedge into a boatyard. Bearing right, walk through to follow a track out to a lane. The Duke's Head lies just to the left. ●

Iken and Tunstall Forest

		GPS waypoints	
Start	Snape Maltings		TM 391 575
Distance	8 miles (12.9km)	Ⓐ	TM 393 572
Approximate time	3½ hours	Ⓑ	TM 400 562
Parking	The Maltings car park. If busy in summer, alternative start at Iken Cliff picnic site Ⓑ	Ⓒ	TM 411 559
		Ⓓ	TM 411 551
		Ⓔ	TM 406 547
Refreshments	Pub, restaurant and tearoom at Snape Maltings	Ⓕ	TM 401 542
		Ⓖ	TM 385 562
Ordnance Survey maps	Landranger 156 (Saxmundham), Explorer 212 (Woodbridge & Saxmundham)		

The ingredients of this walk are simple: an outward leg on a path along the shore of a reed-fringed estuary, the return on a forest track. This straightforward description overlooks features such as the fascinating history of Snape, its ancient bridge and the Maltings, which have been transformed into one of the finest concert venues in Europe. The area is, of course, inseparable from the name of Benjamin Britten, who caught its atmosphere in his haunting music.

 Leave the Maltings car park near steps on the sea wall from which the river trips board. Cross a footbridge and go right, following the perimeter of the complex at the fringe of reed beds. Keep going beyond the impressive Hepworth sculpture *Family of Man* to a junction of paths Ⓐ. Turn left into marshland.

A plank walk and a footbridge takes the path across the head of a creek. After this you may like to divert onto a path that sweeps left through coastal grassland which, as the notice says, is an ideal spot for a picnic. Both paths come together farther on, continuing along another stretch of boardwalk as Iken church comes into view across the

reed beds and a bend of the river. Keep going, eventually passing below *Iken Cliff picnic area and car park, the alternative start if parking is congested at the Maltings* Ⓑ. This is a delightful spot to pause and take in the tranquil beauty of the scene. It is hard to imagine the staithe here being busy

Along the shore of the River Alde

Moorings near Snape Bridge

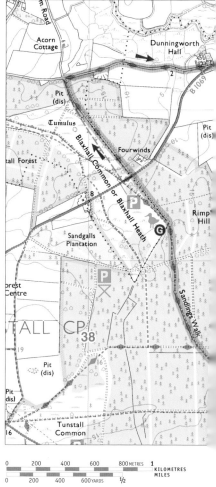

with river traffic in the 18th and 19th centuries, when grain was loaded into barges bound for London. Keep ahead following 'Suffolk Coast and Heaths Path' waymarks to reach a junction of tracks below a house. Bear left on a gravel path past the tiny Jumbo Cottage, the way dropping to run at the edge of the marsh. Farther on the marsh gives way to a sandy beach below a low cliff, which at high water may be washed by the tide for a short time. The path eventually climbs over the flood embankment and through thicket, becoming enclosed to reach a lane **C**.

Go left and then left again at a junction, following the lane to St Botolph's Church at its end. Often visited by pilgrims, it is a wonderful place for quiet reflection and, unlike many remote churches, is always open. It dates from 1450 and has a splendid font that escaped damage from bigots in the 16th and 17th centuries.

Return along the lane, continuing beyond **C** to then turn left down Sandy Lane. Follow it past several pretty cottages for ¹/₂ mile (800m) to a sharp

left bend **D**. Leave there, turning right along a track marked as a footpath, which joins a hedge beside a field of free-range pigs. Reaching the corner of a pinewood, bear right to follow the perimeter, passing through a gap at the far end to meet a farm track **E**.

Keep ahead for another ¹/₃ mile (536m), emerging through a belt of trees onto a lane. Cross to a footpath opposite into Tunstall Forest. After a few steps turn right and then go left, walking for 100 yds (91m) to find a waypost beside a fork **F**. The Suffolk Coast and Heaths Path is indicated ahead, but you should take the lesser, unmarked path off to the

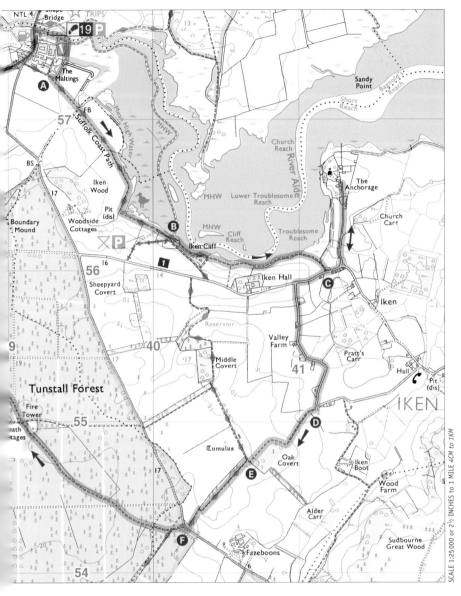

right. After crossing a track, the path broadens, running boldly ahead through the forest and cutting over three other tracks before reaching a junction at Heath Cottages.

Keep ahead, passing beside a barrier and shortly arriving at a fork. Leave the main track, which bends away to the right, walking forward again when you reach a crossing track and subsequently, a skewed path. The way then soon reaches a lane. Cross to continue with the ongoing track over Blaxhall Heath, bearing right in a small clearing when it divides **G**.

Cross another road to the track opposite and follow a dilapidated rabbit fence, the soft sand underfoot defying an energetic pace. The way finally ends at a junction of lanes. Turn right, later joining the main road to Snape, which to the left leads back to the Maltings. ●

Wenhaston and Mells from Blythburgh

Start	Blythburgh	GPS waypoints	
Distance	8¼ miles (13.3km)	✐	TM 450 752
Approximate time	3½ hours	Ⓐ	TM 441 747
		Ⓑ	TM 423 758
Parking	Church car park (donations, please park away from the church on Sundays)	Ⓒ	TM 413 756
		Ⓓ	TM 405 769
Refreshments	Pubs at Blythburgh, Wenhaston and Blyford	Ⓔ	TM 424 764
		Ⓕ	TM 434 761
Ordnance Survey maps	Landranger 156 (Saxmundham), Explorer 231 (Southwold & Bungay)		

The route begins at Holy Trinity, one of Suffolk's great churches, which stands beside the site of a former Augustinian priory. The way follows little frequented field and waterside paths to explore the wild and beautiful course of the River Blyth and countryside just to the south of Halesworth.

✐ Turn left out of the church car park and left again down Church Lane past the church. Imposing enough from the outside, Holy Trinity is quite spectacular within. It boasts a massive nave into which sunlight floods from a dramatic run of clerestory windows. Lift your eyes even higher and there is a magnificent hammerbeam roof, its spans and panels still richly coloured with original paint. From the apex of each rafter an angel looks down upon the congregation, a full dozen in all. Sacrilegiously, they are peppered with lead shot, apparently as a result of someone trying to get rid of jackdaws roosting in the rafters. The church is also noted for its collection of medieval poppy heads, the beautiful carvings decorating the pew ends, although the pews themselves are 'modern', replaced in the 19th century. Amongst the intriguing carvings, you will find

representations of the seven deadly sins: gluttony with a well-rounded belly and sloth lounging in bed. Another interesting feature is the 17th-century Jack-o'-the-clock at the east end, which used to strike the hours.

Follow Church Lane around the bend and look for a narrow footpath to the right just before a white cottage. This leads to a bank, the former track of the Southwold to Halesworth Railway, which operated from 1879 to 1929. To the left, it leads to Wenhaston Lane. There, go right, walking for ⅓ mile (536m) to find a footpath signed off through a gate on the right Ⓐ. Strike diagonally across the field to a stile below an oak tree in the far corner, maintaining the same line across the angle of the next field to a waymarked narrow gap in the bottom hedge. Keep ahead at the field edge on a developing track, which crosses a ditch before

Blythburgh church

swinging left to Laurel Farm. Negotiate a stile and then a gate to enter the farmyard and bear right to leave along a track, which eventually becomes metalled approaching Wenhaston.

At a junction with the main street opposite St Peter's Church, go right to walk through the village. Ignore the first fork, but after ¼ mile (400m), bear off left along Coles Hil Ⓑ. Swing left at the bottom past the Wesleyan Chapel, continuing on a short track to a lane. Cross to a tarmac track opposite, Wash Lane, soon leaving at a waymark onto

an old hollow way on the right. Emerging at the corner of a field, carry on beside a tree-lined ditch to meet another lane.

Go left past Bartholomew's Farm, leaving just after the yard through a signed gap in the right hedge Ⓒ. Follow the hedgerow away, crossing a stile in the corner to continue on its other flank. Entering the next field bear right, skirting the end of a tree-fringed ditch to proceed with the boundary on your right. Some 20 yds (18m) beyond a gate, turn through a tunnel-like gap in the hedge. Walk away to a kink in the hedgerow, crossing a plank bridge into the adjacent field. Strike across to a

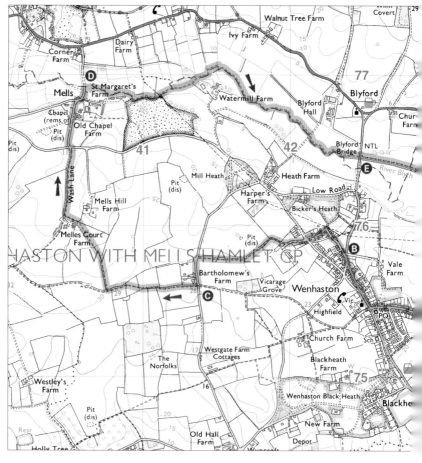

0   200   400   600   800 METRES   1
                                                 KILOMETRES
                                                 MILES
0   200   400   600 YARDS   ½

the church at Blyford comes into view
and it is then not long before you reach
Blyford Bridge **E**.

The Queen's Head Inn is just a short
walk to the left, but the way back
continues by the river in the next
meadow over the stile diagonally
opposite. Beyond another stile in the far
corner, the path runs along the top of a
low flood embankment. The landscape
now acquires an air of wilderness as the
banks become reedy and the meadows
give way to grazing marsh. Rustling
fronds and the cry of the curlew might
be the only sounds to be heard and the
river itself becomes lost behind the tall
grass. Eventually the path leads to a
bridge **F**.

The large building on the nearby

bridge in the far right corner by a low
brick building. Over that go left and
then right, heading down beside
another Wash Lane at the edge of a golf
course. Emerging at a crossroads follow
the lane opposite signed to Holton,
keeping right at the next junction and
winding around to a bridge across the
River Blyth **D**.

Take the waymarked concrete path
immediately after it past a gauging
station and cross a stile into the
meadow behind. Walk away beside the
river from field to field, later passing
through a wood to continue at the edge
of lush grazing once more. Eventually

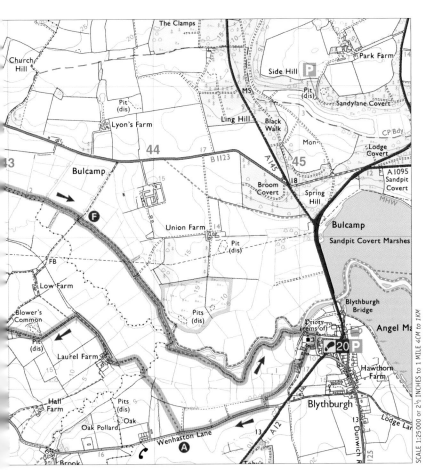

SCALE 1:25 000 or 2½ INCHES to 1 MILE 4CM to 1KM

hillside is the former Blything Union Workhouse, built in 1766 to house the poor and destitute of the area. At one time it housed more than 350 people, who were employed on a variety of tasks including tending the extensive garden and working on the adjoining farm as well as producing linen, woollen cloth and knitted goods. At first, discipline was lax and by all accounts the inmates lived well, but the regulations were later tightened, the perks abolished and the sexes strictly segregated. Like many other old workhouses, it eventually became a hospital, providing long-term care for the chronically sick. That too eventually closed and, at the start of the 21st century, conversion to residential accommodation gave it a new lease of life.

Cross the river, continuing along its southern bank. Before long, the course of the river becomes increasingly meandering, the path sometimes parting from the main flow beside fragmenting drainage channels. Blythburgh's church beckons from its island of higher ground, but for a long time it never seems to be any closer. Eventually, however, the path arrives below the church at a small clearing in the reeds, which serves as a landing. Leave the river at this point on a rising path tunnelling through thicket, emerging by the angel war memorial at the east end of the church. The car park is just to the right. ●

Barham, Baylham and Coddenham

		GPS waypoints
Start	Gipping Valley Centre, Barham Picnic Site	
		🖉 TM 123 512
Distance	8 miles (12.9km)	Ⓐ TM 121 509
Approximate time	3½ hours	Ⓑ TM 112 526
		Ⓒ TM 130 542
Parking	Car park at start	Ⓓ TM 141 532
Refreshments	Pubs at Barham and Coddenham. Refreshment is also available at Baylham Rare Breeds Farm in season	Ⓔ TM 143 527
		Ⓕ TM 131 526
		Ⓖ TM 127 523
Ordnance Survey maps	Landranger 156 (Saxmundham), Explorer 211 (Bury St Edmunds & Stowmarket)	

Few country walks come better than this one. The Gipping valley features at the beginning, where you see a lovely watermill and perhaps kingfishers or even an otter. Then a path through woodland climbs out of the valley over fields and meadows to Coddenham, an attractive and unspoilt village.
The way back is on field paths and through the park of Shrubland Hall, a spectacular Victorian mansion. Note that the route encounters the busy A14 and, although there is a central refuge, care is required in crossing.

🖉 Leave by the Gipping Valley Information Centre and toilets, following a sign to the River Path past the picnic and play areas. Cross the road, descending to a path and walking left below the embankment. Turn right through a gap onto a track by a lake, unromantically called Barham B Pit, and then go left at the end on a causeway to join the riverbank by a railway bridge Ⓐ.

Head upstream to come out onto a track at Great Blakenham Lock. Cross the bridge and then take the first turning on the right. At the end, go right again along a narrow passageway between houses to regain the river. The

path continues beside the water, later passing back beneath the railway. There follows a particularly beautiful section, with willows and reeds lining the bank and plenty of waterbirds and dragonflies to be seen. Upon reaching Sharn Ford Lock, there is a glimpse of Shrubland Hall and its delicate tower. The lock is one of 16 that were built in 1793 to enable barges to reach Stowmarket, 17 miles (27km) upstream from Ipswich. But with the advent of the railways, traffic declined and by the 1920s it had become disused, with the lock gates being replaced by weirs to maintain water levels in the reaches.

Passing a small car park and bridge

leading to fishing pools, the way meanders on over a stile. Later mount another stile to stay beside the water, which winds past the Baylham Rare Breeds Farm where exotic sheep and goats graze on the other side of the river. Cross a bridged ditch and then, farther on, a stream, the path soon ending at a lane beside a mill **B**. Note the pretty carved heads on either side of its doorway lintel. The mill was one of 12 along the navigable stretch of the Gipping and the millwrights strongly opposed the building of the locks in order to protect their water supply. It is therefore ironic that a lock was built beside the mill, this one still with the

remains of the original gate. The place has been a river crossing since at least Roman times and was controlled by a small fort on the eastern bank, Combretovium.

Over the bridge, keep ahead past the entrance to the Rare Breeds Farm to follow the Gipping Valley Circular Path along Mill Lane, disused since it was severed by the construction of the main road. Steps lead down to the busy A14 and, as traffic moves quickly, wait for a long gap in the flow before crossing each carriageway. Climb the embankment on the other side and continue over the old Norwich Road to a pleasant woodland track opposite.

Coddenham church

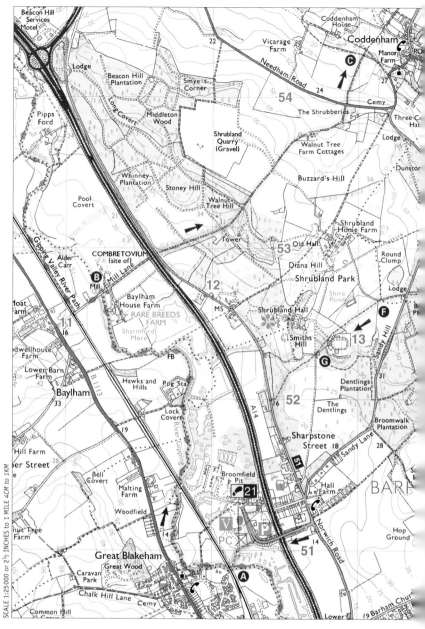

After a crossways overlooked by a tower the track climbs more steeply before breaking out from the trees.

Keep ahead on a hedged track and later, over a junction, Coddenham coming into view as the way then falls. When the track meets a road, cross to a path opposite that follows a hedge to a footbridge and carries on down the side of another field. Over a stile **C**, turn right, crossing a meadow to the drive from Coddenham House, which to the right, leads to a road.

The village and pub lie to the left, but the ongoing route enters the churchyard. The church is notable for its fine double hammerbeam roof embellished with angels looking down upon the nave, which is entered by a porch, oddly skewed to face the village.

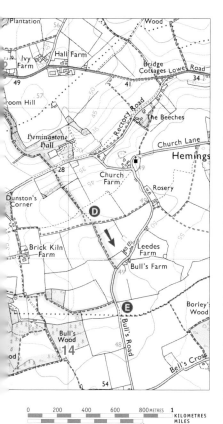

out to Bull's Road.

Turn right and after 200 yds (183m) take a signed footpath off on the right **E**. Cross a narrow field to the end of a hedge, continuing with it to the corner of a wood. Over a ditch, carry on within the fringe of the trees, leaving to follow a ditch on your right. Skirt another coppice and wind on at the field edge, passing a redundant stile into the next field. Through a gap at the far side, keep going to the far-right corner, passing through thicket to a stile. Keep ahead at the edge of another wood to a stile by a pink bungalow and turn left along its driveway. Keep right as another track joins to emerge onto a lane opposite an entrance to Shrubland Park.

Follow the drive from the lodge for 200 yds (183m) to a bend, there leaving over a stile on the left **F**. Strike a right diagonal across the park to the far boundary, turning right beside it past a redundant stile to meet a drive by the stables. Shrubland Hall lies over to the right and was originally built in the Classical style by James Paine in 1770. Seventy years later Sir Charles Barry transformed it into the extravagant Italianate mansion we see today. Until recently it was the home of the Lord de Saumarez and run as a health clinic, but the settlement of death duties forced its sale in 2006.

Walk on along a path that drops below the stables to a remarkably ornate timber lodge **G**. Over a cattle-grid, leave at a footpath sign, bearing right across the park. Keep to the right of a deep pit, passing below ornamental iron gates. Picking up more fingerposts, skirt left around the far side of the pit and then bear right, a developing path taking you through trees out of the park onto a road. Go left to pass The Sorrel Horse Inn before turning right to cross a bridge over the A14 and return to the Gipping Valley Centre. ●

Leave through a kissing-gate in the south east corner. Walk on at the edge of a paddock to another kissing-gate at the foot of Broom Hill, land bought by the village in 1988. Follow a path at the lower edge of the wood, passing south-facing seats beneath oak trees that make a good place to rest. The path eventually joins a drive from a house to reach a road.

Cross to a path opposite, worn hollow by many generations of travellers who once toiled uphill by the side of pack animals, and climb a stile at the top. Pause to look back at Hemingstone Hall, a beautiful Jacobean house built of red brick, but largely hidden by trees in summer. Continue on a broad grassy track towards a farm in the middle distance. Where the track ends, go left beside a ditch as far as a plank bridge **D**, from which a field edge path leads

Stowlangtoft and Norton from Pakenham

		GPS waypoints	
Start	Pakenham church		TL 930 670
Distance	9¼ miles (14.9km)	**Ⓐ**	TL 932 671
Approximate time	4 hours	**Ⓑ**	TL 940 671
Parking	Church car park	**Ⓒ**	TL 944 684
Refreshments	Pubs at Norton and Pakenham	**Ⓓ**	TL 946 689
Ordnance Survey maps	Landranger 155 (Bury St Edmunds), Explorer 211 (Bury St Edmunds & Stowmarket)	**Ⓔ**	TL 959 695
		Ⓕ	TL 959 685
		Ⓖ	TL 953 661
		Ⓗ	TL 938 660

There is much pleasant countryside to enjoy on this walk even though neither of the villages visited is renowned for its church or other ancient building. The landscape is an admirable mix of woodland and farming land that is typical of rural Suffolk.

St Mary's Church at Pakenham is unusual in having transepts, and the cruciform shape and central tower mean that its orientation is not immediately obvious from the outside. The nave is Norman, constructed of material brought all the way from the Barnack quarries near Peterborough, necessitated by the lack of local building stone. The south transept and chancel are Early English, but Teulon remodelled the building during the mid-Victorian period and added the missing transept. The medieval font is outstanding with an impressive cover and faces decorated with carvings of a unicorn, dragon, lamb and pelican.

From the far end of the car park, cut half-right across the churchyard to find a kissing-gate hidden at the end of a flint wall marking its northern boundary. Drop into a meadow and turn right, passing the grounds of Newe House. During the late 19th century, the mansion was home to the village's most colourful character, 'American' Reeve, a local lad who eloped with his sweet-

heart and made his fortune across the Atlantic. He returned home a rich man and astounded everyone by immediately buying the estate. Reeve remembered his humble beginnings and showed great generosity to the poor but he also brought his American ways to Pakenham, dressing as a cowboy and shooting tin cans with deadly accuracy to the great amusement of the village boys.

Go right to another gate at the corner by a tennis court in the neighbouring garden, from which a path strikes across the fields to woodland **A**. Keep ahead

at a fingerpost through a belt of trees, walking on beyond along a field-edge path beside Pakenham Wood. A lovely view opens up as you fork left around the corner, continuing beside the wood to another junction **B**. Turn right on a bridleway heading for a large green shed, built on the site of Beaumont's Hall.

Bear left with the main track around the buildings and then past a pond, keeping left again at a fork to reach Bull

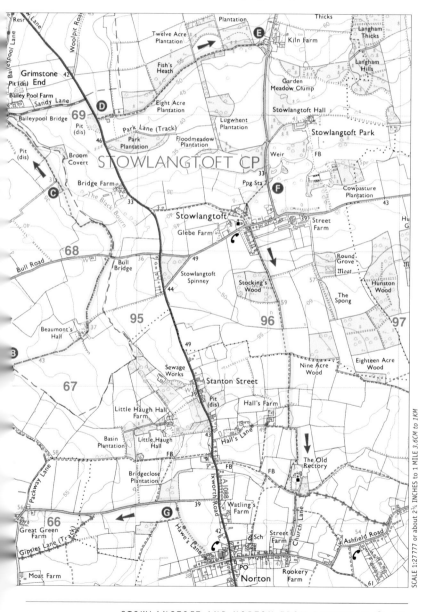

SCALE 1:27777 or about 2½ INCHES to 1 MILE 3.6CM to 1KM

Road. Cross to a footpath on the other side, bordering the convoluted field edge to a stile. Cut across the top end of a small meadow and keep ahead over a crop field to the corner of a reservoir embankment on the far side **Ⓒ**. Through a gap, the footpath then follows the edge of a meadow before slipping through the hedgerow to continue with it on your right.

Reaching Sandy Lane, turn right to cross the Black Bourn and continue up to the main A1088 road. Go right again, leaving after 200 yds (183m) along a farm track on the left **Ⓓ**. Pass above a deep chalk pit to a junction and bear right, the track winding on past a cottage and then beside woodland at the edge of open fields. A lovely section follows with views of woodland to the right, the track finally ending near a picturesque thatched cottage onto a lane opposite Kiln Farm **Ⓔ**.

Turn right, in a while passing the Victorian Stowlangtoft Hall, now a nursing home. Towering Wellingtonia stand around the entrance of its drive and there is a view across the park to the ivy-covered house with its Italian-style tower. Carry on over a bridge then leave through a kissing-gate on the

St Mary's Church

right beside a small pumping station **Ⓕ**. Cut diagonally across to a stile and follow an enclosed path into the village by the church. St George's was built by Robert Davey, who died in 1401, and inside is some superb wood carving and a large wall painting of St Christopher. Turn left to the main street, crossing to a track by the side of Christmas Cottage.

Follow the track past Stocking's Wood, continuing ahead beyond its end across the middle of a field. Through a gap at the far side, turn left and then right within the corner, carrying on to meet a track by Hall's Farm. Keep going along a path almost opposite, passing through a bridged gap in the next corner. Go left and right to remain in the field, but later slip through the boundary to continue on its opposite flank. Just before reaching the end, pass back through the hedgerow and head diagonally across a small field. Walk out along a broad grassy track past The Old Rectory and then St Andrew's Church, swinging left at the bottom to meet Church Lane. Walk down to its end and turn right through the village to reach a junction with the main road by The Dog pub.

Cross into Heath Road, leaving that right along Hawe's Lane, a narrow byway that twists through fields to meet a lane **Ⓖ**. Turn left and follow it for about one mile (1.6km). Keep ahead past the road off to Tostock but then turn right immediately after down Poplar Farm Lane. As it shortly swings right beyond a cottage, go through an opening on the left **Ⓗ** and walk away beside the right-hand hedge. The onward path, clearly marked by wayposts, winds repeatedly right and left at the edge of successive fields, eventually settling towards Packenham church. Ultimately emerging past cottages onto a lane, turn right back to the car park entrance. ●

Denham Castle and the three churches

		GPS waypoints
Start	Packhorse Bridge, Moulton	🖊 TL 697 645
Distance	9¼ miles (14.9km)	Ⓐ TL 712 627
Approximate time	4 hours	Ⓑ TL 722 621
Parking	Close to the bridge	Ⓒ TL 726 623
Refreshments	Pubs at Moulton, Dalham and Gazeley	Ⓓ TL 731 633
		Ⓔ TL 741 628
Ordnance Survey maps	Landranger 155 (Bury St Edmunds), Explorer 210 (Newmarket & Haverhill)	Ⓕ TL 746 637
		Ⓖ TL 719 642

Allow plenty of time for this enjoyable ramble, since there are three beautiful churches as well as the same number of pubs along the route. Denham Castle, a Norman motte was built to command a wide area, and its elevated position certainly offers wonderful views across the north Suffolk countryside.

In the 15th century the River Kennet must have been a much more formidable stream than it is today and the beautiful Packhorse Bridge at Moulton would not have appeared misplaced. Today it looks stranded, as there is rarely more than a tiny stream beneath the concrete ford to lap against the piers of the bridge.

🖊 Walk southwards by the trickle along Brookside, passing other bridges that take footpaths into the village. The lane finally ends beside St Peter's Church. A field track takes the way on above the river, now screened within scrub, but to the left is a typical Suffolk landscape of large fields interspersed with clumps of trees. The Icknield Way Path is claimed to follow the oldest road in Britain, running for 105 miles (169km) between Ivinghoe Beacon in Buckinghamshire and Knettishall Heath in Norfolk, and little imagination is needed to picture a packhorse train or

team of oxen ambling along it.

Reaching a lane, turn right to cross Catford Bridge and then look for a footpath on the left Ⓐ into the wood. This soon leads to another field-edge path rising along the gentle valley, giving a glimpse ahead to the sail-less cap of a windmill. Eventually the path becomes contained and swings back across the tiny stream over a white bridge into Dalham. The pub lies a short way to the right, but the onward route takes you left, passing an unusual bottle-shaped brick malt kiln opposite a road climbing to the church.

Just beyond the kiln, turn right onto a footpath across the park Ⓑ that runs through an avenue of horse chestnuts up to the church. To its left and built in 1704, Dalham Hall was the childhood home of the South African Statesman, Cecil Rhodes. St Mary's Church had a spire, which fell during a great storm that swept England on the night of

Oliver Cromwell's death in 1658.

Turn right to pass the church and then fork left along the drive towards Garden House, leaving left after 200 yds (182m) onto a waymarked path into the trees **C**. There are occasional glimpses to the church and hall before the path cuts through the wood to run at its eastern edge. Waymarks guide you through the fringe of Brick Kiln Wood, crossing the edge of open ground into Blocksey Wood. Continue along the perimeter path, turning left and right at successive corners. Where the path bends left for the second time, keep

ahead at a waypost, emerging over a plank bridge onto the edge of a field **D**. Go right along the boundary, towards Desning Hall Farm. There is an outstanding view northwards towards Thetford Forest.

Walk right and wind between barns, turning right again to leave the yard. Reaching a 'Private' sign at the edge of fields, go left onto a bridleway. Although not quite the highest spot in Suffolk, the vast fields and wide sky give a rare feeling of isolation. Here, some 40 miles (64km) from the coast, the hills are nearly 350ft (106m) high, but only 10

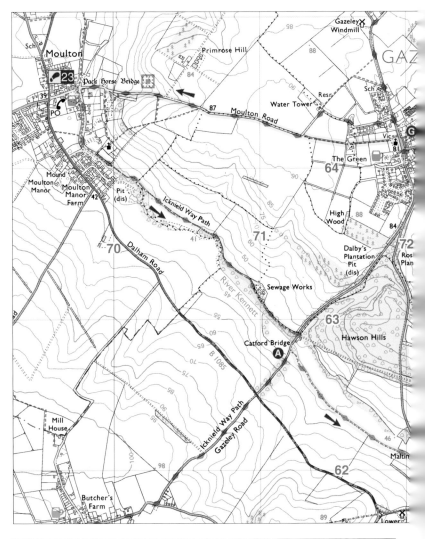

miles (16.1km) or so to the north west the fenland is hardly above sea level.

Reaching the corner of a wood, keep ahead along its edge, passing through a gap into another field. Go left to the corner and into the adjacent field **E**, turning to walk with the hedge on your right. At the next corner swing left, continuing at the far side along an enclosed path that skirts the motte-and-bailey of Denham Castle. The earthwork encloses a considerable area, the castle mound rising at the northern point. The site was occupied by a Saxon lord long before the Normans arrived. However,

the fortifications seen today date from the 12th century, when the country was divided by civil war after Stephen seized the throne from his cousin, Empress Matilda on the death of her father, Henry I.

Through a kissing-gate, head down the left-hand side of a field beside an orchard, dropping out at the bottom onto a lane by Castle Cottages. Turn left along the quiet byway for ³⁄₄ mile (1.2km), bearing left at a Y-junction to

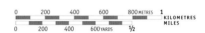

descend a hill. Where the lane bends sharply right, look for a bridleway on the left **F**. Follow the field-edge away, bearing left at a fork into the adjacent field. This is another lonely part of the walk where you are likely to have only partridges for company. The path shortly swaps to the other side of the hedge, eventually joining a tarmac track that climbs to meet a lane at Desninghall Cottages. At the telephone box go left and wind back through the farmyard, retracing your outward steps along the field edge and returning to Blocksey Wood **D**.

In the trees, turn right to rejoin the Icknield Way Path, which twists in and out of the woodland fringe as before.

After crossing a footbridge, Gazeley church comes into view, the path continuing between fields. Keep going across a final pasture to an enclosed path that emerges between houses onto the village green. Cross to an asphalt path and follow it left, keeping right at a fork onto Higham Road.

Go left to the village centre and turn right past the church, leaving along a footpath bounding the north side of the churchyard **G**. Keep forward over a drive past paddocks, eventually passing through a hedge onto Moulton Road. Ahead it leads back to Packhorse Bridge.

The unusual malt kiln in Dalham

Kersey and Lindsey Castle from Hadleigh

		GPS waypoints	
Start	Toppesfield Bridge, Hadleigh		TM 025 421
Distance	9½ miles (15.3km)	**A**	TM 015 418
Approximate time	4 hours	**B**	TM 006 426
Parking	Near bridge	**C**	TL 982 443
Refreshments	Pubs at Kersey	**D**	TL 985 432
Ordnance Survey maps	Landranger 155 (Bury	**E**	TL 992 428
	St Edmunds), Explorer 196	**F**	TM 000 426
	(Sudbury, Hadleigh & Dedham	**G**	TL 999 414
	Vale)	**H**	TM 006 407
		J	TM 014 407

The walk between Hadleigh and Kersey is a well-established and waymarked route over some lovely countryside. The second part of this expedition will take you on paths that are far less frequented but deserve to be better known.

Although the walk leaves Hadleigh from the ancient Toppesfield Bridge spanning the River Brett, the town itself is also worth exploring for its wealth of medieval and later buildings. Many of these are grouped around St Mary's Church, including the 15th-century guildhall, which was once used as a school, and the Deanery Tower, all that remains of Archdeacon Pykenham's palace built in 1495.

From the western side of the bridge take the concrete track rising beside the farm. Fork right when this divides, soon reaching Park Farm. Bear left to continue up the hill at the field edge to a junction of tracks **A**. Turn right, signed to Coram Street, along a delightful broad green way, lined by fine trees and from which there is a wonderful vista to the north. Meeting a lane by Coram Lodge Farm, go left and then left again at the main road. After 100 yds (91m) look for a waymarked track off on the right **B**. Kersey church

can be seen in the middle distance before the path later drops steeply into Kersey Vale.

At the bottom, join a track away from Vale Farm. Keep to the main route between the fields, bearing left at the top to pass a row of cottages. Go forward at two successive junctions towards Kersey Street, the lane then dropping below the church. St Mary's has overlooked the steep valley since well before the *Domesday Book* was compiled, although much of the present building is from the 14th and 15th centuries. Inside are fragments of medieval wall painting and some fine examples of plaster and stonework. However, the labours of the masons undertaking the decoration were disrupted when plague afflicted the village in 1384.

The view across the village as you head downhill to the ford is perhaps one of the prettiest in all of Suffolk. A delightfully haphazard assortment of ancient half-timbered and thatched cottages lines the single street, which climbs away beyond the stream past The Bell to a bend at the top in front of an old village pump.

Leave there and keep ahead up a footpath, turning left at its end onto a lane. It leads past the private grounds of Priory Farm, where there are remnants of the large church that once served an Augustinian monastery founded in the early 13th century. Walk along the peaceful lane for a mile (1.6km) to reach Seagers Cottage **C**. Immediately after, a footpath on the left crosses a plank bridge over a stream. The brook watered the moat of Lindsey Castle, a stronghold that straddled it just upstream to the right, but whose extensive earthworks are now hidden within the trees and undergrowth. Built by the Normans, the castle was still in use in c 1150 at the end of their era.

The ongoing footpath strikes southwards across the middle of successive open fields, eventually emerging onto a narrow lane coming from Bridges Farm **D**. Follow it right into the hamlet of Kersey Tye, there following signs left and left again towards Kersey.

Keep left at the next junction and then go along the Polstead road on the right by an attractive thatched cottage. Walk to a right-hand bend by Hart's Farm and take the track off on the left **E**. After ¼ mile (400m) the pleasant green way opens into a field. Follow a grass path to the left, keeping ahead past the corner to drop across the field to a hedged ditch **F**. Turn right beside it for 300 yds (274m) and then look for a waymarked bridge across. The onward path climbs at the edge of the field, after a while becoming an enclosed track that ends at the main road.

Turn right along the verge towards Hadleigh Heath, crossing after 150 yds (137m) into a quiet lane signed to Polstead. As the lane shortly bends right

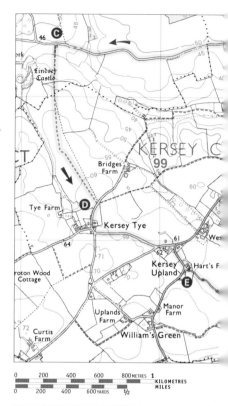

after the telephone box, a footpath is signed off through a gap on the left **G**. It winds around a garden to a field, continuing along its left-hand boundary. Go over a narrow lane and carry on beside a hedge, crossing a footbridge at the bottom. Keep ahead across the field beyond towards an oak tree, turning left to emerge onto another lane. Walk right for 50 yds (46m) to find a track leaving on the left **H**.

The pleasant grass track winds across the farmland, meeting a tarmac drive at Rands Farm. Turn left, but as it then swings into the yard, leave right along a greensward to pass at the field side of a shed. Beyond, a delightful sunken way falls into the wooded valley, where it leads onto a boardwalk across the marshy bottom at the head of a small lake **J**.

The causeway curves left to firmer ground, where steps climb a bank to a stile above. Keep ahead, rising at the edge of a field. Meeting a crossing path,

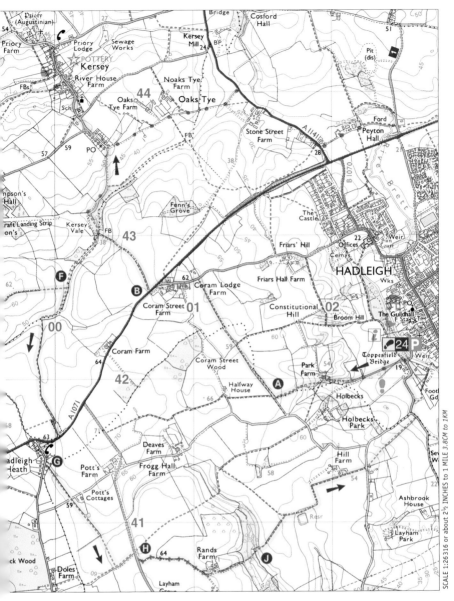

dog-leg right and left to maintain your forward progress along a grass way that winds between open fields, its course marked by sporadic oaks. There is a beautiful panorama across the undulating countryside and, although we often complain about Suffolk's lack of hedges, there are indeed places where they would screen a wonderful landscape. Keep ahead at a fingerpost to wind past a small irrigation reservoir, after which, the track bends left. Leave the track at the top of the field, turning right beside a high hedge that screens Hill Farm. At the far end, follow the drive away from the farm to meet a lane. Cross to a signed footpath opposite and strike a left diagonal straight down the field, joining the right-hand hedge lower down to emerge at the bottom corner onto another lane. Turn left and then at a junction, right, to pass a large sports ground and return to Toppesfield Bridge. ●

The Shotley Peninsula

		GPS waypoints	
Start	Shotley	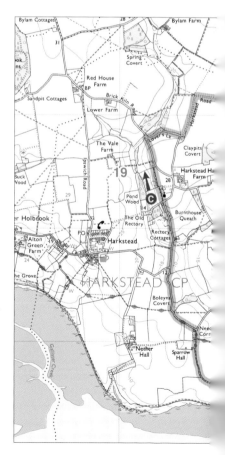	TM 235 350
Distance	10¼ miles (16.5km)	**A**	TM 235 341
Approximate time	4½ hours	**B**	TM 199 334
Parking	Village hall car park	**C**	TM 193 352
Refreshments	Pubs at Shotley, Harkstead,	**D**	TM 204 373
	Chelmondiston and Pin Mill	**E**	TM 229 373
Ordnance Survey maps	Landranger 169 (Ipswich & The	**F**	TM 233 366
	Naze), Explorer 197 (Ipswich,		
	Felixstowe & Harwich)		

The shoreline of the River Stour is much less frequented than that of the Orwell on the northern side of the Shotley Peninsula but it is hardly less delightful. There are several pubs to visit on the way but it might be a mistake to make the lengthy walk into a crawl!

Shotley village hall is on the B1456 next to The Rose pub. Turn right onto the main road and after 100 yds (91m) go right again through the yard of Rose Farm. A straight and hedgeless track strikes south towards the River Stour, passing a cottage with tall chimneys. Turn right at the shore **A** to pass behind Rose Farm cottages.

Carry on along a field-edge path above the salt marshes of Erwarton Bay. There are views of Harwich and its busy North Sea ferries. Closer to, the tidal fringes are a paradise for a variety of waders and other birds feeding off the rich mud flats and the romantic, plaintive call of the curlew is a common sound over this lonely countryside. Rounding Erwarton Ness, the slim tower of the Royal Hospital School at Holbrook comes into view ahead. Soon afterwards the way drops to Johnny All Alone Creek, a wonderful name commemorating some long-dead marshman. About ½ mile (800m) farther on the path passes through a tall hawthorn hedge **B**. Turn right to head inland beside it, bearing left at the top to join a track that eventually meets a lane at Needle Corner.

Turn left and keep ahead at the next junction, *unless you wish to take refreshment at the pub in Harkstead, about ½ mile (800m) down the lane. If you do this you can subsequently rejoin* the main route at Harkstead church. Either way, when you reach the church, look for a stile to the left of the letterbox at the end of the churchyard wall **C**.

Follow the field edge beside the

Awaiting high tide at Pin Mill

church, passing through a gate in the corner. Cross a stile in front, from which a fenced path runs between paddocks. Follow the right edge of the field beyond, leaving right when you reach a crossing track onto the adjacent lane. Turn left and then at the bottom, go right along Lover's Lane. Reaching a T-junction with Harkstead Road, follow it left for a mile (1.6km) to Chelmondiston.

The village pub lies about 200 yds (183m) to the right, but unless you wish to pay it a visit, turn off left almost immediately into Woodlands. Walk past a school and then abandon the road for a bridleway on the right. Meeting another street go right again, but just before the junction in front of the church, turn left onto a bridleway ⓓ signed to Pin Mill.

Over a stile at the end, walk down to the bottom of a lovely meadow from which there are views of the River Orwell. Over successive stiles at the end of a contained path keep ahead beside another wetland meadow. Leave over a stile opposite a boatyard. Pass beside it to the waterfront where The Butt and Oyster and Pin Mill lie just to the right. Although more usually associated with the Lake District, the famous author and newspaper correspondent, Arthur Ransome, also lived here at Pin Mill for a while, incorporating the riverside setting in two of his books, *The Big Six* and *We Didn't Mean to Go to Sea*.

Climb away past the Pin Mill Studio and then the entrance to a car park and picnic site, looking for a stepped path leaving on the left. Cross a drive at the top to an ongoing path that passes between bungalows before winding left around paddocks into the National Trust's Pin Mill Wood. Keep ahead, following waymarks for the Suffolk Coast and Heaths trail, along a popular and beautiful path that undulates through the trees along the coast. Emerging at the far side of the wood, skirt the shoreward side of a white cottage to follow a path atop a low embankment looking out across the marshes to the River Orwell. Continue beyond at the edge of fields, later crossing a footbridge and duck-boarded way and eventually passing through a hedge to reach a timber-clad chalet ⓔ.

Turn beside it away from the coast, climbing along a broad grass path to Orwell Cottages. Through a gate, keep ahead on a rising gravel track to meet a lane. Go left, passing Charity Farm to then turn right at Upper Lodge onto a track marked as a cycleway ⓕ. It leads between the fields, giving views of the rows of gantry cranes, used to unload the container ships at Harwich Docks, before reaching Shotley church. Although it looks quite modern from afar, it is in fact a medieval building. Bear right past cottages to a junction of lanes by the church. Take the one ahead which dips into a valley before climbing to the main road. Turn right to return to the village hall in Shotley. ●

Go right and then almost immediately left along Harp Lane, waymarked as the Stour Valley Path. Beyond the police station, it degrades to a track, passing a chicken house and continuing as a path through a long thicket. Emerging onto the edge of a field, follow it left to the corner near Hermitage Farm **Ⓐ**. Head right and climb beside the hedge, pausing to look back for a good view of Clare.

Turn left at the top and continue with the hedge on the left. After the path then swings right there is a fine panorama with the farm at Houghton Hall in front. Cross a track and keep ahead past the yard, walking in the field beyond with the boundary on your right. Halfway along, slip through a wide gap, following the other side of the hedge to the bottom of the field. Go right, reaching a footbridge across the ditch, some 300 yds (274m) along. On the other bank, swing right and left over a smaller bridge to head away with the ditch on your left.

Turn right onto a lane, abandoning it after ¼ mile (400m) at the second left-hand bend for a footpath on the right

Ⓑ. It takes a pleasantly meandering route around field edges, eventually passing another path signed off to the left. Ignoring it, keep ahead, but after another 300 yds (274m) cross a plank bridge and continue on the opposite flank into the corner. Entering a meadow, follow its boundary around left, leaving on a contained path that winds beside a cemetery to Cavendish village green by the school. Walk past the school and The Five Bells to the church, from where the scene is as typically Suffolk as you might get, with church, pub and pretty colour-washed cottages surrounding a pleasant green. The village is the 14th-century ancestral home of the Cavendish family, the Dukes of Devonshire, whose family seats are at Chatsworth in Derbyshire and Bolton Abbey in Yorkshire.

Walk through the churchyard to find a footbridge at its north east corner. A passageway leads to a field, the path running on at the back of house gardens. Leaving them behind the way rises over a gentle hill between large cultivated fields, occasional oak trees standing as the only testimony to lost hedgerows.

The George in Cavendish

Dropping to a hedge at the far side **C** go right leaving the field halfway along through an opening onto an adjacent farm track. To the right it becomes metalled and soon passes Ducks Hall Farm. Deserting the lane at a footpath sign on the left immediately beyond the yard **D**, cross the edge of the hardstanding and climb steps behind a barrel-roofed shed into a field.

Accompany the hedge left, continuing beyond the corner across the field, aiming for a pink cottage on the skyline. Crossing a ditch, maintain the same heading over a smaller field to a green lane. Turn right to Cavendish Lanc and go lcft, climbing for 300 yds (274m) to find a signed path leaving through a wide opening on the right **E**. Walk away with the hedge initially on your right, passing onto the other side towards the far end. Carry on in the subsequent field, the wonderful views extending to Pentlow Tower as the path descends. Turn left at the end of the hedge to follow the track uphill, going right at the top to the next corner **F**.

Glemsford, where there are a couple of pubs, is only a few minutes' walk away. To reach it, continue along the track to a junction. Go left past cottages but almost immediately turn off in favour of a field-edge path on the right, which emerges between cottages onto the main street.

Otherwise, leave the track on the corner **F**, turning right to drop across two small fields in the direction of distant Cavendish church. Through a gap and stile in the hedge, follow the boundary around to more stiles in the far-left corner.

A grassy path continues ahead between the fields towards the village, the path later dog-legging right and left and eventually reaching a four-way signpost in the middle of a field **G**. Turn left, pass through a gap and continue across a playing field to Melford Road.

Follow the lane opposite over Pentlow Bridge, walking for another ¼ mile

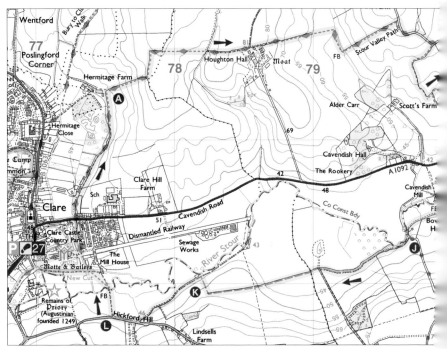

(400m) to a junction . Turn sharply right onto a bridleway, which runs away at the field edge along the valley of the meandering River Stour. After a while it passes through thicket and then beside open fields once more, ultimately reaching Bower Hall. Beyond, the way becomes metalled and before long leads to a pumping station by a bend **J**.

Turn off there onto a wooded bridleway above the river, keeping ahead when it later emerges at the edge of successive fields. The track eventually swings right towards the river, meeting a gravel track **K**. Follow it left to a road and there go right. After 200 yds (183m), look for a signed path on the right **L**. Walk down to a footbridge over the River Stour and then strike left towards the far corner. Cross an overflow weir and continue beside the channel that was dug to feed the former mill. Reaching the old girder railway bridge, cross back to the starting point.

Long Melford from Lavenham

Start	Lavenham	**GPS waypoints**	
Distance	12¾ miles (20.5km)	🔲 TL 913 489	
Approximate time	5½ hours	**A** TL 900 490	
		B TL 876 491	
Parking	Car park opposite church	**C** TL 860 493	
Refreshments	Pubs and tearooms at Lavenham	**D** TL 860 485	
	and Long Melford, pub at Bridge	**E** TL 848 479	
	Street	**F** TL 844 472	
		G TL 845 460	
Ordnance Survey maps	Landranger 155 (Bury	**H** TL 864 468	
	St Edmunds), Explorer 196	**J** TL 871 472	
	(Sudbury, Hadleigh & Dedham	**K** TL 882 473	
	Vale)	**L** TL 890 481	
		M TL 906 488	

This is a classic Suffolk walk, starting from one of the county's most picturesque market towns and visiting another. Both have magnificent churches as well as a wealth of beautiful old houses, and there are two historic houses on the route: Melford and Kentwell halls.

Lavenham is one of the most perfect of English villages with its array of timber-framed houses and a wonderful church reflecting the great wealth generated by the medieval cloth industry. Flemish weavers settled here in the 14th century and the town developed a reputation for its 'Lavenham Blue' cloth. The 15th-century church, dedicated to St Peter and St Paul, demonstrates the town's prosperity at that time and has been described as a miniature cathedral. It is said that the 141ft (43m) tower would have been even higher had the mason not fallen from the top. Such was the trade that three separate guildhalls were built, the most notable being the Guildhall of Corpus Christi overlooking the market place. It has been used as a prison, workhouse, almshouse and store and is now in the care of the National Trust. The fine building contains a

fascinating exhibition describing the town's history and there is a beautiful walled garden containing plants grown to produce dyes for the cloth.

🔲 Leaving the car park by The Cock, head left to the church. Walk through the churchyard and descend steps by the tower to a lane. To the right it winds past a farm to reach Park Road. Turn left and, after ¼ mile (400m), go left again onto the trackbed of an old railway line that once linked Lavenham with Sudbury via Long Melford.

This is a popular path with birdwatchers and there are occasional seats where one can relax and look for the woodpeckers that inhabit the surrounding woodland. Walk for a little over ½ mile (800m) and, immediately under a bridge, climb a path on the right **A** to leave the railway for the road. Turn left along the lane, which gives views over a wide swathe of countryside.

The lane descends to the main road at Bridge Street. Cross to the byway beside The Rose and Crown Inn, soon turning off right onto Aveley Lane. After 100 yds (91m) take the footpath on the left **B**, just before a line of houses set back from the road. The pleasant field path continues beyond the end of a hedgerow and across the subsequent field to a waypost by an oak tree. Pass through the hedge and go left, striking from the corner to a break between two copses.

The ongoing path skirts Ashen Grove and then Kiln Grove, developing as a track that leads to a junction near Kiln Farm **C**. Turn left along a straight avenue of sporadic oaks that takes the bridleway towards another wood. At a junction there **D**, go right to join the Stour Valley Path. A wide path follows the edge of the wood and is delightful country walking. Keep left with the corner and accompany the hedge from field to field, eventually reaching a waymark. Bear away from the boundary towards the foot of the field, leaving

through a gap near the right corner. Continue at the edge of a long meadow, bypassing farm sheds and a yard to reach the B1066 at Cranmore Green. Follow the road right for 200 yds (183m) before turning left onto an enclosed path by Mill Farm **E**. It leads to a footbridge over the little River Glem. Bear right across a meadow to another footbridge and then climb ahead to meet the corner of a hedgerow.

Walk forward but after a few steps, slip through the hedge onto its other side. At the corner, go left on a grass path that soon swings right across a final field, joining a track beside a bungalow to reach a T-junction **F**. Turn left, cross a gravel driveway and follow posts around the edge of a wooded lawn to a bridge. Pass through a small thicket and carry on at the edge of a meadow to a lane.

Go right and, at the end, cross the main road to a footpath almost opposite that climbs within a broad hedge. Finally breaking out, continue in the same direction with the hedge on your right. Turn left at the bottom of the field **G** and follow a fence to meet a track. To the

Lavenham's magnificent church

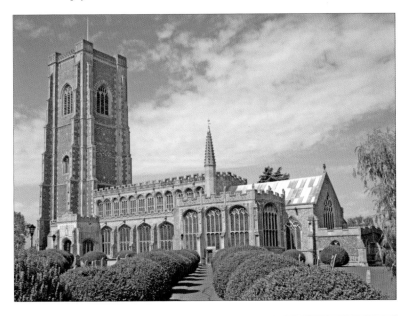

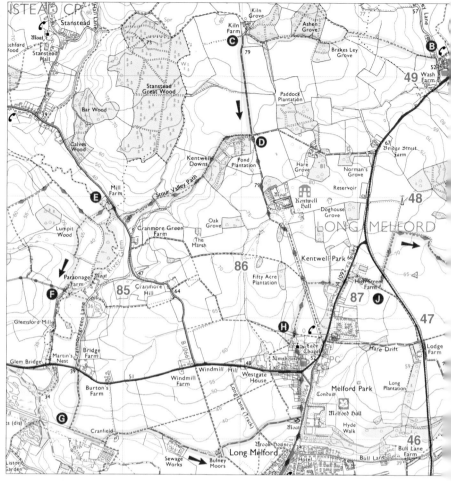

left, it swings past a thatched cottage, Cranfield, joining a concrete track, which later passes a small water treatment works. Carry on along a field track and then a green lane that emerges in Long Melford at the southern end of the green by the attractive Victorian school.

Turn left towards the church, passing a row of elegant Georgian houses facing Melford Hall on the other side of the green beyond the main road. The hall, dating from 1559, is one of Suffolk's finest Elizabethan buildings and was built for Sir William Cordell, Speaker of the House of Commons. At the top of the green is The Black Lion and beyond, the magnificent Holy Trinity Church. In *The Buildings of England* Long Melford church is described as 'one of the most

moving parish churches of England, large, proud and noble'. As at Lavenham, its furnishings, monuments and architecture testify to the wealth generated by the cloth trade. Inside, the Clopton Chantry is a remarkable monument to one of the most prosperous of these medieval entrepreneurs and makes a fitting climax to visiting this church of outstanding beauty. Beside it stands the Trinity Hospital, also built and endowed by Sir William, about fifteen years after the completion of the hall.

Walk through the churchyard and past the tower, taking the drive towards the rectory. Where it swings right, keep ahead over a stile behind a telegraph post and follow a fence for 20 yds (18m)

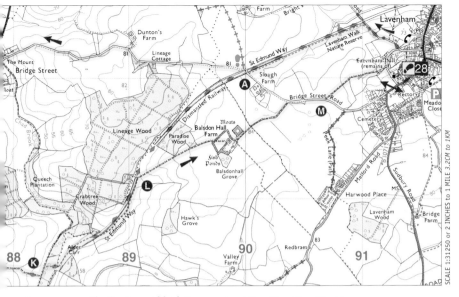

SCALE 1:31250 or 2 INCHES to 1 MILE 3.2CM to 1KM

to a squeeze stile. Cross a paddock to another stile in the far corner and pass through a belt of trees to emerge at the edge of Kentwell Park **H**. Keep on a beaten path across the park to a stile on the far side and turn left onto an avenue of impressive limes, planted in 1678. Almost a mile (1.6km) long, it is the grand approach to Kentwell Hall, a moated house four years older than Melford Hall and hardly less impressive, although the interior was remodelled after a fire in 1822.

Leave after 50 yds (46m) over a stile on the right, making for a belt of tall trees. Breaking out beyond onto uncultivated ground, carry on along a clear path that curves towards houses to reach the main road.

Go left, but after 100 yds (91m), take a footpath on the right, briefly following the field edge away behind the houses before crossing the adjacent ditch onto a track from High Street Farm. Go right for about 200 yds (183m) and then turn left **J**, crossing the field to a stiled gap in the far hedge onto the main road. Cross with care to a path opposite and walk away at the field edge. At the top, as a radio mast comes into view, turn within the field corner. Follow the

hedge a few yards before swinging through a gap to continue with the boundary then on your right, eventually reaching a wood at the bottom **K**.

Turn left, looking for a path into the trees after 150 yds (137m). Drop over a bridge spanning Chad Brook, climbing to the edge of a meadow beyond. Bear left and walk away with a small wood on the right, once more following the course of the old railway line. The way later passes through trees, eventually reaching a junction at the edge of open ground **L**. Follow the track right, curving past the tip of Paradise Wood to Balsdon Hall Farm. The track winds across the former moat, now partly obscured by vegetation, and then by farm sheds to a junction. Go left passing another shrouded earthwork, Lavenham church tower coming into view as you walk out to a lane. Go right and after ¼ mile (400m) take a field path on the left **M** that leads across a couple of fields to meet your outward route at the edge of Lavenham. Turn right, retracing your steps to the church and the start of the walk. ●

Further Information

The National Trust

Anyone who likes visiting places of natural beauty and/or historic interest has cause to be grateful to the National Trust. Without it, many such places would probably have vanished by now.

It was in response to the pressures on the countryside posed by the relentless march of Victorian industrialisation that the trust was set up in 1895. Its founders, inspired by the common goals of protecting and conserving Britain's national heritage and widening public access to it, were Sir Robert Hunter, Octavia Hill and Canon Rawnsley: respectively a solicitor, a social reformer and a clergyman. The latter was particularly influential. As a canon of Carlisle Cathedral and vicar of Crosthwaite (near Keswick), he was concerned about threats to the Lake District and had already been active in protecting footpaths and promoting public access to open countryside. After the flooding of Thirlmere in 1879 to create a large reservoir, he became increasingly convinced that the only effective way to guarantee protection was outright ownership of land.

The purpose of the National Trust is to preserve areas of natural beauty and sites of historic interest by acquisition, holding them in trust for the nation and making them available for public access and enjoyment. Some of its properties have been acquired through purchase, but many of the Trust's properties have been donated. Nowadays it is not only one of the biggest landowners in the country, but also one of the most active conservation charities, protecting 581,113 acres (253,176 ha) of land, including 555 miles (892km) of coastline, and over 300 historic properties in England, Wales and Northern Ireland. (There is a separate National Trust for Scotland, which was set up in 1931.)

Furthermore, once a piece of land has come under National Trust ownership, it is difficult for its status to be altered. As a result of parliamentary legislation in 1907, the Trust was given the right to declare its property inalienable, so ensuring that in any subsequent dispute it can appeal directly to parliament.

As it works towards its dual aims of conserving areas of attractive countryside and encouraging greater public access (not easy to reconcile in this age of mass tourism), the Trust provides an excellent service for walkers by creating new concessionary paths and waymarked trails, maintaining stiles and footbridges and combating the ever-increasing problem of footpath erosion.

For details of membership, contact the National Trust at the address or telephone number on page 95.

The Ramblers' Association

No organisation works more actively to protect and extend the rights and interests of walkers in the countryside than the Ramblers' Association. Its aims are clear: to foster a greater knowledge, love and care of the countryside; to assist in the protection and enhancement of public rights of way and areas of natural beauty; to work for greater public access to the countryside; and to encourage more people to take up rambling as a healthy, recreational leisure activity.

It was founded in 1935 when, following the setting up of a National Council of Ramblers' Federation in 1931, a number of federations in London, Manchester, the Midlands and elsewhere came together to create a more effective pressure group, to deal with such problems as the disappearance or obstruction of footpaths, the prevention of access to open mountain and moorland, and increasing hostility from landowners. This was the era of the mass trespasses, when there were sometimes violent confrontations between ramblers and gamekeepers, especially on the moorlands of the Peak District.

Since then the Ramblers' Association has played a key role in preserving and developing the national footpath network, supporting the creation of national parks and encouraging the designation and waymarking of long-distance routes.

Our freedom of access to the countryside, now enshrined in legislation, is still in its early years and requires constant vigilance. But over and above this there will always be the problem of footpaths being illegally obstructed, disappearing through lack of use, or being extinguished by housing or road construction.

It is to meet such problems and dangers that the Ramblers' Association exists and represents the interests of all walkers. The address to write to for information on the Ramblers' Association and how to become a member is given on page 95.

Walkers and the Law

The Countryside and Rights of Way Act (CRoW Act 2000) extends the rights of access previously enjoyed by walkers in England and Wales. Implementation of these rights began on 19 September 2004. The Act amends existing legislation and for the first time provides access on foot to certain types of land – defined as mountain, moor, heath, down and registered common land.

Where You Can Go
Rights of Way
Prior to the introduction of the CRoW Act, walkers could only legally access the countryside along public rights of way. These are either 'footpaths' (for walkers only) or 'bridleways' (for walkers, riders on horseback and pedal cyclists). A third category called 'Byways open to all traffic' (BOATs), is used by motorised vehicles as well as those using non-mechanised transport. Mainly they are green lanes, farm and estate roads, although occasionally they will be found crossing mountainous area.

Rights of way are marked on Ordnance Survey maps. Look for the green broken lines on the Explorer maps, or the red dashed lines on Landranger maps.

The term 'right of way' means exactly what it says. It gives a right of passage over what, for the most part, is private land. Under pre-CRoW legislation walkers were required to keep to the line of the right of way and not stray onto land on either side. If you did inadvertently wander off the right of way, either because of faulty map reading or because the route was not clearly indicated on the ground, you were technically trespassing.

Local authorities have a legal obligation to ensure that rights of way are kept clear and free of obstruction, and are signposted where they leave metalled roads. The duty of local authorities to install signposts extends to the placing of signs along a path or way, but only where the authority considers it necessary to have a signpost or waymark to assist persons unfamiliar with the locality.

The New Access Rights
Access Land
As well as being able to walk on existing rights of way, under the new legislation you now have access to large areas of open land. You can of course continue to use rights of way footpaths to cross this land, but the main difference is that you can now lawfully leave the path and wander at will, but only in areas designated as access land.

Where to Walk
Areas now covered by the new access rights – Access Land – are shown on Ordnance Survey Explorer maps bearing the access land symbol on the front cover.

'Access Land' is shown on Ordnance Survey maps by a light yellow tint surrounded by a pale orange border. New orange coloured 'i' symbols on the maps will show the location of permanent access information boards installed by the access authorities.

Restrictions
The right to walk on access land may

Countryside Access Charter

Your rights of way are:

- public footpaths – on foot only. Sometimes waymarked in yellow
- bridleways – on foot, horseback and pedal cycle. Sometimes waymarked in blue
- byways (usually old roads), most 'roads used as public paths' and, of course, public roads – all traffic has the right of way

Use maps, signs and waymarks to check rights of way. Ordnance Survey Explorer and Landranger maps show most public rights of way

On rights of way you can:

- take a pram, pushchair or wheelchair if practicable
- take a dog (on a lead or under close control)
- take a short route round an illegal obstruction or remove it sufficiently to get past

You have a right to go for recreation to:

- public parks and open spaces – on foot
- most commons near older towns and cities – on foot and sometimes on horseback
- private land where the owner has a formal agreement with the local authority

In addition you can use the following by local or established custom or consent, but ask for advice if you are unsure:

- many areas of open country, such as moorland, fell and coastal areas, especially those in the care of the National Trust, and some commons
- some woods and forests, especially those owned by the Forestry Commission
- country parks and picnic sites
- most beaches
- canal towpaths
- some private paths and tracks Consent sometimes extends to horse-riding and cycling

For your information:

- county councils and London boroughs maintain and record rights of way, and register commons
- obstructions, dangerous animals, harassment and misleading signs on rights of way are illegal and you should report them to the county council
- paths across fields can be ploughed, but must normally be reinstated within two weeks
- landowners can require you to leave land to which you have no right of access
- motor vehicles are normally permitted only on roads, byways and some 'roads used as public paths'

lawfully be restricted by landowners. Landowners can, for any reason, restrict access for up to 28 days in any year. They cannot however close the land:

- on bank holidays;
- for more than four Saturdays and Sundays in a year;
- on any Saturday from 1 June to 11 August; or
- on any Sunday from 1 June to the end of September.

They have to provide local authorities with five working days' notice before the date of closure unless the land involved is an area of less than five hectares or the closure is for less than four hours. In these cases landowners only need to provide two hours' notice.

Whatever restrictions are put into place on access land they have no effect on existing rights of way, and you can continue to walk on them.

Dogs

Dogs can be taken on access land, but must be kept on leads of two metres or less between 1 March and 31 July, and at all times where they are near livestock. In addition landowners may impose a ban on all dogs from fields where lambing takes place for up to six weeks in any year. Dogs may be banned from moorland used for grouse shooting and breeding for up to five years.

In the main, walkers following the routes in this book will continue to follow existing rights of way, but a knowledge and understanding of the law as it affects walkers, plus the ability to distinguish access land marked on the maps, will enable anyone who wishes to depart from paths that cross access land either to take a shortcut, to enjoy a view or to explore.

General Obstructions

Obstructions can sometimes cause a problem on a walk and the most common of these is where the path across a field has been ploughed over. It is legal for a farmer to plough up a path provided that it is restored within two weeks. This does not always happen and you are faced with the dilemma of following the line of the path, even if this means treading on crops, or walking round the edge of the field. Although the later course of action seems the most sensible, it does mean that you would be trespassing.

Other obstructions can vary from overhanging vegetation to wire fences across the path, locked gates or even a cattle feeder on the path.

Use common sense. If you can get round the obstruction without causing damage, do so. Otherwise only remove as much of the obstruction as is necessary to secure passage.

If the right of way is blocked and cannot be followed, there is a long-standing view that in such circumstances there is a right to deviate, but this cannot wholly be relied on. Although it is accepted in law that highways (and that includes rights of way) are for the public service, and if the usual track is impassable, it is for the general good that people should be entitled to pass into another line. However, this should not be taken as indicating a right to deviate whenever a way becomes impassable. If in doubt, retreat.

Report obstructions to the local authority and/or the Ramblers' Association.

 Global Positioning System (GPS)

What is GPS?

GPS is a worldwide radio navigation system that uses a network of 24 satellites

and receivers, usually hand-held, to calculate positions. By measuring the time it takes a signal to reach the receiver, the distance from the satellite can be estimated. Repeat this with several satellites and the receiver can then use triangulation to establish the position of the receiver.

How to use GPS with Ordnance Survey mapping

Each of the walks in this book includes GPS co-ordinate data that reflects the walk position points on Ordnance Survey maps.

GPS and OS maps use different models for the earth and co-ordinate systems, so when you are trying to relate your GPS position to features on the map the two will differ slightly. This is especially the case with height, as the model that relates the GPS global co-ordinate system to height above sea level is very poor.

When using GPS with OS mapping, some distortion – up to 16ft (5m) – will always be present. Moreover, individual features on maps may have been surveyed only to an accuracy of 23ft (7m) (for 1:25000 scale maps), while other features, e.g. boulders, are usually only shown schematically.

In practice, this should not cause undue difficulty, as you will be near enough to your objective to be able to spot it.

How to use the GPS data in this book

There are various ways you can use the GPS data in this book.

1. Follow the route description while checking your position on your receiver when you are approaching a position point.

2. You can also use the positioning information on your receiver to verify where you are on the map.

3. Alternatively, you can use some of the proprietary software that is available. At the simple end there is inexpensive software, which lets you input the walk positions (waypoints), download them to the gps unit and then use them to assist your navigation on the walks.

At the upper end of the market Ordnance Survey maps are available in electronic form. Most come with software that enables you to enter your walking route onto the map, download it to your gps unit and use it, alongside the route description, to follow the route.

 Walking Safety

Although the reasonably gentle countryside that is the subject of this book offers no real dangers to walkers at any time of the year, it is still advisable to take sensible precautions and follow certain well-tried guidelines.

Always take with you both warm and waterproof clothing and sufficient food and drink. Wear suitable footwear, such as strong walking boots or shoes that give a good grip over stony ground, on slippery slopes and in muddy conditions. Try to obtain a local weather forecast and bear it in mind before you start. Do not be afraid to abandon your proposed route and return to your starting point in the event of a sudden and unexpected deterioration in the weather.

All the walks described in this book will be safe to do, given due care and respect, even during the winter. Indeed, a crisp, fine winter day often provides perfect walking conditions, with firm ground underfoot and a clarity unique to this time of the year. The most difficult hazard likely to be encountered is mud, especially when walking along woodland and field paths, farm tracks and bridleways – the latter in particular can often get churned up by cyclists and horses. In summer, an additional difficulty may be narrow and overgrown paths, particularly along the edges of cultivated fields. Neither should constitute a major problem provided that the appropriate footwear is worn.

 Useful Organisations

The Broads Authority
18 Colegate, Norwich NR3 1BQ.
Tel. 01603 610734
www.broads-authority.gov.uk
Broads Authority information centre (open Easter to October):
Beccles: 01502 713196

Campaign to Protect Rural England
128 Southwark Street, London SE1 0SW.
Tel. 020 7981 2800
www.cpre.org.uk

Camping and Caravanning Club
Greenfields House, Westwood Way, Coventry CV4 8JH.
Tel. 0845 130 7633 (site bookings)
www.campingandcaravanningclub.co.uk

Forest Enterprise England
340 Bristol Business Park, Coldharbour Lane, Bristol BS16 1EJ.
Tel. 0117 906 6000
www.forestry.gov.uk
District Office: East Anglia
Santon Downham, Brandon, Suffolk IP27 0TJ.
Tel. 01842 810271

Long Distance Walkers' Association
www.ldwa.org.uk

Council for National Parks
6-7 Barnard Mews, London SW11 1QU.
Tel. 020 7924 4077
www.cnp.org.uk

National Trust
Membership and general enquiries:
PO Box 39, Warrington WA5 7WD.
Tel. 0870 458 4000
www.nationaltrust.org.uk
East of England Regional Office:
Westley Bottom, Bury St Edmunds Suffolk IP33 3WD.
Tel. 01284 747500

Natural England
Head Office, 1 East Parade, Sheffield S1 2ET.
Tel. 0114 241 8920
www.naturalengland.org.uk
Enquiry Service (Peterborough)
Tel. 0845 600 3078

Ordnance Survey
Romsey Road, Southampton SO16 4GU.
Tel. 08456 05 05 05
www.ordnancesurvey.co.uk

Further Information

Ramblers' Association
2nd Floor, Camelford House,
87–90 Albert Embankment,
London SE1 7TW.
Tel. 020 7339 8500
www.ramblers.org.uk

Suffolk County Council
Endeavour House, 8 Russell Road,
Ipswich IP1 2BX.
Tel. 01473 583000
www.suffolk.gov.uk

Tourist information:
East of England Tourist Board,
Toppesfield Hall, Hadleigh,
Suffolk IP7 5DN.
Tel. 0870 225 4800
www.visiteastofengland.com

Local tourist information offices
(*seasonal):
Aldeburgh: 01728 453637
*Beccles: 01502 713196
Bury St Edmunds: 01284 764667
Felixstowe: 01394 276770
*Flatford: 01206 299460
Ipswich: 01473 258070
*Lavenham: 01787 248207
Lowestoft: 01502 533600
Newmarket: 01638 667200
Southwold: 01502 724729
Stowmarket: 01449 676800
Sudbury: 01787 881320
Woodbridge: 01394 382240

Youth Hostels Association
Trevelyan House, Dimple Road,
Matlock, Derbyshire DE4 3YH.
Tel. 0870 770 8868
www.yha.org.uk

Weather forecasts:
Weathercall (Met office forecast by phone)
Tel. 09014 722058

Ordnance Survey Maps of Suffolk

The area of Suffolk is covered by
Ordnance Survey 1:50 000 (1¼ inches to
1 mile or 2 cm to 1km) scale Landranger
map sheets 134, 143, 144, 154, 155, 156,

Sutton Hoo

168 and 169. These all-purpose maps are
packed with information to help you
explore the area. Viewpoints, picnic sites,
places of interest and caravan and
camping sites are shown, as well as public
rights of way information such as
footpaths and bridleways.

To examine the Suffolk area in more
detail and especially if you are planning
walks, Ordnance Survey Explorer maps at
1:25 000 (2½ inches to 1 mile or 4cm to
1km) scale are ideal:

196 Sudbury, Hadleigh & Dedham Vale
197 Ipswich, Felixstowe & Harwich
210 Newmarket & Haverhill
211 Bury St Edmunds & Stowmarket
212 Woodbridge & Saxmundham
226 Ely & Newmarket
229 Thetford Forest in The Brecks
230 Diss & Harleston
231 Southwold & Bungay

The Explorer map OL40 (The Broads), at
1:25 000 scale, is also helpful.

To get to the Suffolk area use the
Ordnance Survey OS Travel Map-Route
Great Britain at 1:625 000 (1 inch to
10 miles or 4cm to 25 km) scale or the OS
Travel Map-Road 5 (East Midlands and
East Anglia including London) at
1:250 000 (1 inch to 4 miles or 1cm to
2.5km) scale.

Ordnance Survey maps and guides are
available from most booksellers, stationers
and newsagents.

www.totalwalking.co.uk

www.totalwalking.co.uk
is the official website of the Jarrold
Pathfinder and Short Walks guides. This
interactive website features a wealth of
information for walkers – from the latest
news on route diversions and advice from
professional walkers to product news, free
sample walks and promotional offers.

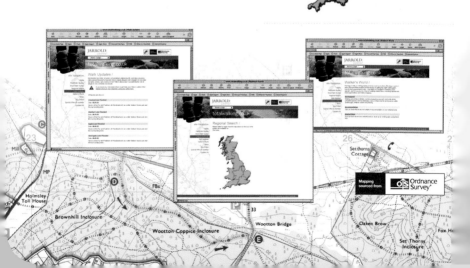